CAN PLANNING BE DEMOCRATIC ?

A Collection of Essays prepared for
the Fabian Society

by

HERBERT MORRISON, M.P., T. W. AGAR
BARBARA WOOTTON, C. E. M. JOAD
JOAN ROBINSON AND G. D. H. COLE

GW00729066

VORA & CO., PUBLISHERS LTD.
3, ROUND BUILDING, BOMBAY, 2.

CONTENTS

THE STATE AND INDUSTRY

By THE RT. HON. HERBERT MORRISON M. P.

MY approach to this subject is that of a Socialist who has lost none of his former faith but is persuaded of the need of re-thinking and re-shaping political conviction in relation to contemporary fact. My analysis of the new forces at work in our economic life does not point away from those conclusions that I accepted in the early days of my political and economic education. It simply enables me to re-state them in terms of the practical politics of to-day. Instead of a prophetic vision only, I now see also a table of priorities ; instead of a flight of imagination, I tend to keep my feet on the ground. But I do not think the inward significance of my creed is different from what it was, and I suspect that its practical effectiveness may be greater.

For in Britain we have pinned our faith to government by consent. Democracy means that you must carry a majority of the people with you, and if the changes you want to make are great and sweeping ones it had better be something more than a bare majority. This seems a simple and obvious thing to say, but it is too often overlooked by the idealogues. To suggest that, having set out your programme, your subsequent failure to win consent and adherence is merely a failure of propaganda may well be a complete fallacy. The roots of propaganda must be embedded deep in the programme, and I have seen superficially attractive and intellectually beguiling programmes that were in fact barren soil.

So when we turn our minds to this fundamental question of the State and Industry, let us keep close to the hard-headed, practical common-sense of the average British man and woman, who may not be good at political ideology in the Continental manner but who know very well when a shoe pinches and will listen to an honest craftsman telling them what has to be done, even if it means a specially made last and a good deal of re-fashioning.

This question of the relation between Industry and the State I call fundamental. Of course there are all sorts of fundamental questions in politics. If I were in another vein to-day I might with good reason call foreign policy fundamental, or education, or full employment, or civil liberty. But we live in an age when the unsolved problems of industrial organisation seem to have a greater power to wreck our societies and to bring our political aspirations to naught than any other single factor. We live too in an age when the solution to these problems offers greater and more appealing prospect than ever before in history, of lifting man above the crippling hardship of unsatisfied physical need which has dogged him throughout his history. So for to-day and in a very real sense the problem of industry is my fundamental one.

· When we look back over the history of modern industry, that is, in Britain, industry since the Napoleonic wars, we see an obvious trend from the small to the large in organisation. We see too a trend away from competition and towards co-operation in various forms. Not that I think that the picture drawn by the individualist economists ever really obtained in practice. The perfect competition of Adam Smith, in which every producer fought his rivals to the death and the consumer throve on the debris of battle, was never more than a myth—significant of one aspect of the early phase in industry, but a distortion of many of its other aspects. Every man who could get away with his own little monopoly, whether he was a country storekeeper or a Midland brass founder with a new invention, got away with it. Even Adam Smith knew that if half a dozen business men got together to talk about the weather it would not be five minutes before they found themselves discussing how to keep prices up. But the novelty of the new industrial techniques, the then backwardness of communications, the absence of large-scale power transmission in the forms in which we know it, all combined to keep industry small, while the boundless opportunities of the market at home and abroad kept the minds of entrepreneurs from turning in the direction of restrictive alliances. That was the plain homespun meaning of nineteenth-century economics before the economists picked it up and tricked it out in all the bright colours of individualist theory.

From the start the seeds of combination were inherent in the revolutionised industry of the nineteenth century. It is perhaps truer, and more fruitful for our present-day purposes, to think of modern industrial history as a progress towards centralisation, than it is to think of the competitive beginnings as a natural norm and every sign of the spread of combination as an aberration or disease.

To-day we see around us in Britain a fairly advanced
stage in this combining and centralising progress. It
is not as advanced as it was in Germany between the
wars—an interesting sidelight on the power of national
circumstance and character in accelerating an industrial process so that the younger economy outdistances
the older. On the other hand, the process of combination has in many respects gone further here than
in the United States of America, not merely because
we are an older country but because they are so huge
a one. With them, even when modern technology has
nourished great aggregations of plant, capital and skill,
the market is so vast that there has thus far been
room for several great firms competing against one
another, with some genuineness, within the same field
of industry. Moreover, in America, where native
British individualism was strengthened by the pioneer-
ing traditions of the frontier and stamped profoundly
into men's minds in the white-hot fires of the Revolution, they have continued to use legal means to restrain
or impede the combining tendency for longer and with
more success than we have.

In Britain, over a large and growing part of productive and distributive industry, we now find
ourselves confronted by associations and combinations
of some sort. It is desirable that we should understand just what it is that we are talking about when
we speak of this combining and centralising tendency.
I give you a list not pretending to be exhaustive but
throwing its net over a considerable part of the territory with which we have to deal. Beginning with the
least solid forms of combination and going on to the
most solid, we have first associations of manufacturers

or distributors for the regulation of prices—which means in practice of course the maintenance of minimum scales. Then We have, in those trades which have had to deal with depression or declining markets, associations for the regulation, which is to say the restriction, of output. This takes us a stage further because the effect of such agreement cuts deeper into the structure and methods of each individual business. One stage on again is the type of association which allots a given volume of orders in some agreed proportion among its members. Yet one step further is the group which gets together to pool selling ideas and resources, organising a joint monopoly of sorts in the field of commercial development and distribution. In Germany there used to be a special and still more advanced form of this, in which a joint sales syndicate was maintained by an association or cartel members participated to some extent in one another's shareholdings and profits.

I am now moving on from forms of commercial to forms of organic or structural combination. There is the combine built upon an exchange of shares among the members ; there is the form achieved by interlocking directorates, in which the centralised power is in the hands of a number of elusive individuals the pattern of whose activities may take quite a lot of tracing through the columns of the Directory of Directors. There is the more straightforward and and simple form of the Holding Company—now we are moving very close indeed to the full trust. This last in fact is our final item, the product of the complete financial and administrative consolidation or merger of interests, forming a number of independent companies one solid bloc.

I do not wish to pursue this exposition any further, and I apologise for having bored you with it. I did so simply in order that we should be perfectly clear what we are talking about—not simply this form of business organisation or that, but a widespread and pervasive tendency expressing itself in a considerable variety of different forms at different levels of development.

The law of the land would once have been an obstacle to the operation of many of these forms of combination. It would be an interesting study of the relation between law, opinion and economic fact if we had time to study the process whereby something that would once have been called in a court of law a conspiracy in restraint of trade has become not merely tolerated but accepted, not merely accepted but respectable, not merely respectable but frequently a prime objective and pet of Government policy. Lord Mansfield, a great English judge of the eighteenth century, once delivered judgment that " persons in possession of any articles of trade may sell them at prices as they individually may please, but if they confederate and agree not to sell them under certain prices it is a conspiracy ". Certainly the wheel has come full circle when we reach a stage at which such price-fixing combination is not only not illegal but is facilitated by Government action through the imposition of a bumper tariff to ensure that the combine's price can be high enough.

Indeed, in one respect the state of the law is not only no obstacle to this development in public policy but is a powerful reinforcement to it. A patent law is a necessity for the protection of inventors, but the patent law as it is to-day makes it a simple matter for

basic developments in productive technique to become
the property of a firm or group which will then use
them as a bargaining counter in its relations with some
other firm or group. In due course they reach an
understanding either to pool all their important patents
or to divide the market between them on the basis of
this easily enforceable technical division of productive
methods. This patent situation is of particular interest at a time when the most important thing about new
scientific inventions is not the fundamental idea
produced by some individual or group in a laboratory,
but the long, costly and difficult process of turning it
into a workable industrial technique. These development patents are a powerful instrument of monopoly,
a tremendous weapon in the hands of the larger and
more richly endowed corporations or groups. Their
effects in the stultification of technical enterprise, their
restrictive power, the threat they develop to the future
of smaller industries (and, I may add, smaller countries
like Great Britain) is a potent historical factor working
beneath the surface of events in our time. I wish I
had the chance to go into it to-day more fully. At
present my point is simply that here too we have a
particularly important and revealing example of the
deep-rooted tendencies working in our age towards
centralisation in industry.

Between the two wars the natural process of development was marked or accelerated by a number of
actions of Government—not, I may say, confined to
any one Party. In 1925 and 1926 there were financial
enactments which provided tangible inducements to
firms to amalgamate. In the Acts of 1926 and 1930
affecting the coal-mines, compulsory amalgamation,

output regulation, quotas and minimum prices all
formed part of the implements of administration
forged by the Government and handed over to the
industry for its use. The Agricultural Marketing Acts
of 1931 and 1933 represented the deliberate creation of
producers' monopolies in the field of primary production. In the middle 'thirties it was—or it outwardly
appeared to be—Government initiative which produced
the British Iron and Steel Federation, the new monopolist association of all British producers, formed to
rescue a depressed and declining industry from the
combined consequences of world recession and its own
backwardness. It was provided by the Government
with a tariff to make firm ground beneath its feet and
was encouraged to make international market-sharing
agreements. Shortly before the war another blow was
dealt to the dying frame of competitive industry by
the Cotton Industry Organisation Act.

I do not say which of these steps was right or wrong.
I am talking history—noting a significant phase of
policy. How fast and how far the process would have
gone had peace continued, no one can say. Certainly,
however, it has been swiftly accelerated by the circumstances of war. These circumstances can be
grouped under three headings. There is the fact of
shortage, with its results in the need for the centralised allocation of supplies and concentration of production. There have been in industry a great many
hasty war marriages, in terms of combined administration and integrated operation, for which the
Government read the banns.

Just as important, though less often noticed, is the
fact that over the whole field of primary and secondary

war supplies the sole purchaser is the Government. Obviously productive business, confronted by one monopoly buyer in a perfect position to call the tune, reacts by increasing combination, not necessarily in legal or even in written form, but none the less so in fact. This is not in order to defend itself against the buyer's pressure—for in war-time that is not the relationship—but to solve the sheer technical problems of coping with the buyer's demands.

Then, thirdly, there is the need for greatly increased administrative direction of industry by the Government, acting not as purchaser but as guardian and organiser of the home front. To get the spate of wartime directions and regulations understood and administered the Government has welcomed not merely the existence but the presence at its council tables of trade associations in every industry with which it has dealings. Had they not existed, it would have been necessary to invent them. As a result the position of these associations has been much strengthened, and I have no doubt their dreams and ambitions for the future much stimulated.

All these hard facts of business organisation and administrative necessity have naturally resulted in a development of ideas and theories which, while not new, have reached new levels of precision and boldness during the war. I am thinking particularly of the well-known manifesto of the 120 industrialists. They obviously visualise the whole fact of centralisation, nurtured in peace and forced in war, as something to be extricated intact from the clutches of Government after peace arrives, and maintained and directed by the fostering hand of its own beneficent oligarchs. " Self-government in industry " is the cry. I do not deride it. I only ask what "self" it is that we are to arm with the powers of government.

But before I enter on that ground there is more that I wish to cover. Recently we have had a series of statements from eminent—I will not say from eminent monopolists, but from eminent speakers who felt impelled to plead the monopolist case. I thought that without exception they pleaded very well. There is a strong case for centralisation in modern large-scale industry. If there were not, the historical development that I have reviewed above would never have taken place. Centralised control in its various forms gives some assurance of stability in bad times and gives some assurance of stability in bad times and gives at least the opportunity of planned and constructive development in good ones. It mobilises the resources of an entire industry and makes them available for tasks of research and development. It has enabled industries, half broken by unorganised competition on a falling market, to rehabilitate themselves, improve their methods and serve well the interests both of their home consumers and their country's foreign trade. I do not know if this has happened in very many instances, though it has in some few. In others I am not at all sure of the full opportunities of efficiency afforded by large-scale organisation has been realised in practice, and if, having been realised, they have been passed on fully to the consumer. In some cases I find in my mind a marked reservation of judgment about that. But the case, as a case in terms of the theory of organisation and administration, is a good one.

Indeed, it is better than any of the eminent spokesmen themselves made it out to be. I don't think any
of them put the case from the point of view of the
technician, the manager, the organiser, the scientist,
the intellectual in business. For this man, the sense
of constructive opportunity that springs from membership of a large organisation with an *esprit de corps*
and some positive purposes of its own is a very real
thing. He is a far better worker and a far happier
man in such circumstances than he would be if his
brains and energies were harnessed to the merely
competitive purposes of individual businesses on a
small or moderate scale. I have often talked with
such men and I know their mind. Incidentally, I know
also that they are, as a type, singularly uninterested in
those ownership rights which, to a much larger extent,
preoccupy their Chairmen and Directors. They do
not set much store by shareholders. The claims of
shareholders; the claims of dividends which they may
sometimes think a little inflated, are apt to appear to
many of them as simply obstacles in the way of that
genuine and expanding service to the consumer and
the community which it is the real purpose of their
business lives to give. Some may go so far as to wish
shareholders well out of the way. Be that as it may,
if they are more effective beings in a large centralised
organisation than they would be in a smaller competing one, they are also less effective beings in a large
centralised organisation in private management and
ownership than they would be in the same organisation
in public management and ownership. This type does
not, in practice get much kick or spur out of private
ownership—rather the contrary. If the same is true of

the large mass of workpeople, and I think it is, then
the galvanising effects of such ownership must
obviously be of very limited impact on a very limited
impact on a very limited part of the organisation.

But I am prepared to say that so far as the main
case put by the spokesmen is concerned, I agree far
more than I disagree with it, and if, as I have seen
suggested many of these statements were by way of
reply to some earlier observations of mine, then there
has been a considerable misunderstanding.   I hope
to say something to help clear up this misunderstanding later.   What I want to ask now is, what is to be
the practical upshot if we do accept the case for centralisation as it has been set out?   Some of the spokesmen who have expounded it have offered their suggestions for a better relationship between their organisations and public policy.   In one case they
spoke of a public review and regulation of prices.   In
another, a public registration of agreements into
which these great organisations or associations might
enter with other groups in this country or abroad.
There have been from outside the ranks of the big
organisations themselves, other suggestions such as
the public appointment of Chairmen or Members of
Boards.   Or, in the case not of Trusts but of Associations, the setting up of industrial controls to guide
these associations from the point of view of public
policy.

I am not prepared to dismiss all such suggestions as
of no account. Indeed, I have myself given some
currency to one of them. We have a very varied,
many-sided and complicated problem to deal with.
We shall need to deal with it not at one blow by one

method, but by a variety of methods in a campaign of public policy lasting over many years. L stress that point. The forging of a right relation between the State and industry will be a long business. In some parts of the field of work we may have for a long time to content ourselves with a holding campaign, rejoicing if we do any better than merely mark time. In other parts we may have to make experiments more hopeful than convincing. But the point I do want to make is that if we accept any solution less than full and responsible public management and control, we are running a risk. From the point of view of public policy I believe the whole of the evidence to be in favour of such management, and the whole of the onus of proof to be on those who advocate something less.

Why? What is wrong with centralised management in private hands? What risk do we run by allowing it? Three risks. First, the risk of inefficiency—and this is a risk, though not a certainty. Second, exploitation—the use of a privileged position, even in efficient hands—to line the pocket of one's own proprietors rather than to serve the community as economically and fully as possible. Lastly, the irresponsible exercise of power and influence in the political sphere—and this I rate by far the worst menace of the three.

These problems that confront us are not confronting the world for the first time. Take the case of Germany. For a variety of historical, geographical and economic reasons, Germany, in her modern industrial phase, has been a very highly cartelised country. Concentration and combination went a long

way there, even before the last war, and to all out-
ward appearance they exhibited many of the marks
of success. They were extensive in coal and the heavy
industries and in the last war were used as an implement of public control of these industries for war
purposes. Under the Weimar Republic there was sur-
prisingly little change of policy. The State continued
not only to tolerate but in a general way to encourage
this form of industrial organisation. The great industrial corporations which had worked so closely with
the Imperial Militarist group had lost none of their
power. But the collapse of the German currency had
stirred up a great deal of public resentment against
big business in its current forms, and in 1923 the Re-
pubilc enacted a law "against the misuse of economic
power", the purpose of which was to limit the activities of the big cartels. There was to be a Cartel
Court with a President and four Judges. All agreements affecting supplies or prices were to be in writing, and the Reich Minister for Economic Affairs was
to have the right to appeal to the Court if any such
agreements seemed to him contrary to the public interest. The Court had the power to declare the
agreements void. Without appeal to the Court the
Minister could establish the right of firms to terminate
at once any agreement with a cartel which was held
to be limiting production or supplies or fixing unduly
high prices, or imposing buyers' or sellers' boycotts or
imposing differential prices and conditions of sale.

This appeared an impressive enactment, as no doubt
it was meant to be. It had twenty-three sections. As
I have indicated, they included a considerable number of the suggestions which have been put forward

in this country for dealing with our own problem. In practice it was a complete and absolute dead letter. No significant action of any kind was ever taken under it, and the cartels went on growing and strengthening their position until ten years after the enactment of the law to curb them, came the greatest of their achievements, the crowning triumph of bringing Hitler into power. The trend continued and accelerated under the Nazis and their war-production programme. In the end it became extremely difficult to say whether the Nazis were running industry or industry was running the Nazis, and if on balance we are inclined to give the preponderance of power to the political side, it is merely because the urgent needs of the warlike preparations, towards which they themselves had driven their country, had to override increasingly the purely industrial and commercial interests of the great firms. However we look at it the Nazis and the great cartels increasingly formed a partnership from which every genuine consideration of public interest was excluded as completely as the Pharaohs excluded from their Counsels of State any regard for the hoards of slaves who built the Pyramids.

Nor do I believe that this was wholly due to the special circumstances of world depression or to the inherent beastliness of the Nazi mind and creed. It was in some part—you can't read the history of the early relations between the coal and steel trusts and the Nazis without realising—the terrible Nemesis of irresponsible economic power. If we do not understand this fact we are far from understanding the whole truth about Nazism.

I do not say that any kind of economic organisation

in Britain, however misguided and irresponsible in form, would be likely to turn us into a Nazi State. That would imply a gross misreading of British history and would be a gross libel on the British character. What I do say is that the social and political consequences of such irresponsible power—however shocking this suggestion may seem to the well-meaning and often high-minded men who wield it to-day—are bound to be a corrupting and disintegrating force in the State. It would depend on circumstances whether, if the British people allowed them to continue, they turned our island and our commonwealth into a sordid, commercially minded Imperialism, untinged by any sentiment or sense of mission, or into a hard-shelled, unimaginative, complacent little island growing a thicker skin every year and falling gradually and steadily out of the march of genuine human progress. I cannot see how one or other of these consequences could, in practice be avoided.

But I will not be written down as a pessimist. I have far too much faith in the inherent political wisdom of the British people to suppose that they would allow themselves to drift or be driven very far down such a road. A friend who is a historian has given me an account, which I pass on as I received it, of how early in our constitutional history we showed ourselves aware of the threat to healthy political growth and to our liberties implied in any emergence of a power in the State a little too powerful for the State itself. In the England of the fifteenth century the problems of government and of politics were vastly different from what they are to-day, but the fundamental realities were not wholly different. Just as we have a newly emerging conception of government as a positive and constructive instrument of public well-being, struggling for recognition among the great economic and social forces that have survived from an earlier state of development so, my friend points out, in fifteenth-century England did the sovereign power of the King show signs of establishing itself as supreme over the warring forces of the Barons. In his book, *The Governance of England,* one of our very earliest constitutional writers, Sir John Fortescue, dealt with the problems of that day. One of the most pregnant of his chapters, which has been shown me, is that headed " Here he Showeth the Perils that Might Come to The King by Over-Mighty Subjects ". No doubt Fortescue was thinking of people like Warwick the King-Maker, who aspired to make and unmake monarchs as some later exponents of power have aspired to make and unmake governments. That was the peril then that is the peril to-day—the Over-Mighty Subject.

These vast concentrations of economic power are a political menace, however efficient they may be in their economic conduct. They have within their grasp powers over fields of public well-being and public policy far greater in practice than Parliament itsefl wields in the great majority of its legislation. They can determine the form of our technical development. They can by that means determine the pattern of the national working life and the level of the national livelihood. They can control to a great extent the distribution of purchasing power among classes and groups. They are free, like independent empires, to declare war with other empires at home or abroad, to make peace with them. go down to the very roots of national life and our place to make treaties, to enter into alliances. All these things in ways not obvious to ordinary men at ordinary times, in the world. Organisations in a position to wield such power, whatever their present motives or the current ideals of those responsible for their policy, present democracy with its greatest problem. Either they are our creatures, or else are theirs, and our democratic government is a puppet in their hands.

Of what then do I speak? I speak in some degree of every form of centralised economic institution listed at the outset of this paper, from the price-fixing group to the merger in heavy industry. Each in varying degree, and many in greater degree than might appear on the surface, have the means to exercise the forms of economic and social power to which I have referred. None of them should be left indefinitely outside the effective grasp of public policy.

One particular group of industries which are almost certain to exist in highly organised form after the war are the export industries. Indeed, the State itself may very well encourage organisation among them for the sake of helping them to increase their efficiency. And for another reason too. The state can never disinterest itself in the well-being of the workers in any industry.

I hope that by the world-wide accord of Governments, the International Labour Office may be able to secure minimum wage standards in all countries, so as to prevent that worst of all forms of competition which is based on the abject poverty and misery of the workers in socially backward countries. But suppose that some of our export industries have to compete in difficult markets. Suppose that, whether through the payment of very low wages abroad or for some other reason, it is difficult for an export industry to compete successfully while paying the wages that a developed public opinion and our new standards of social enlightenment come to regard as appropriate for our wage-earning citizens. The position of an industry so suited is a matter of public concern, and public policy must take account of it by one means or another. Here is one special but possibly, in post-war circumtsances, extensive and important type of case where the relationship between the State and industry will need to be particularly close, and the responsibility of the State in some respects particularly marked.

The position of the workers in other types of centrally organised or monopolistic industry may well present problems of another kind. One of the effects of organisation or consolidation in such industries is to provide them with a secure and sheltered market at home. Many of the most enlightened of them share the economic advantages of this position with their working people, as indeed it is right they should. They thus achieve a hold upon the loyalty of the mass of their workers which is sometimes proof against a critical approach by those workers to the weaknesses and defects of their industry from the point of view of broad national policy. Let me make it clear that none of the ideas I have propounded about the dangers of centralisation or monopoly should be taken as implying an attack upon the economic security of their workers. Quite the contrary. The truth is that restrictive practices in industry, though they may not be an immediate threat to the livelihood of the workers immediately concerned, are a threat to economic stability and expansion in the community as a whole,

and may well lead to economic difficulties and political
problems which affect every citizen and every wage-
earner by whomsoever employed.

Now to return to the question of the right relationship between the State and centralised industry.

As I have already said, we have a complicated long-
term job in front of us, and the means of which, and
the times at which, the State may move to ensure a
full alignment between the conduct of these various
organisations and the general interests of the nation
may vary. Let me say at once that in my judgment
the complexity of the task and the time it will take
are no reason at all for not making a start with it as
soon after the war as we reasonably can, and for start-
ing in the right place. The British are ready for speed,
so long as it is speed with order. I feel no doubt that
the only genuinely satisfactory course in some of these
instances of monopoly is to socialise them and, I would
add, to run them on the lines of a public corporation.
In other cases we may be led to find methods of
effective management and operation in the public interest without socialising the whole undertaking at any
rate at the outset. All these public operated industries,
whether socialised or not, should include the natural
monopolies, the "common service industries" and
certain others which, while not bearing that name, play
a fundamental part in our economy.

But let us face the fact that there will be quite a
number of fairly strong central organisations which
are bound to continue without coming under any very
strict or extensive public authority for quite a time
to come. We must do something about them if they
are—and they obviously are—in a position to wield

restrictive influence and protect their members against risk—at the consumer's expense. If the private business man is not prepared to take risk, he can claim no immunity from public guidance and control. In the past I have expressed the rather hesitant opinion that the right thing to do in some of these cases may be to enforce competition by legal change, where the absence of competition is operating unfortunately from the public point of view. I do not know why this very cautious and not very optimistically propounded suggestion should have led some people to suppose that I am an ardent advocate of *laissez-faire* and a firm believer in its virtues. In any case, the course of the argument in this present paper will have disabused them of the idea. What I do feel strongly is that the semi-accident by which restrictive practices, which would be outside the law in America, have been able to be built up under cover of the law in this country, is something deserving of early and zealous attention. Once the law is changed, and the old doctrine of conspiracy in restraint of trade is given new force in relation to private price fixing and other restrictive arrangements, you have made it possible to put the industry which wishes to take such steps in the position of having to justify what it wants to do before public authority, and to prevent any action unless this authority gives specific consent. In some istances again I would not rule out the possibility of allowing certain types of grouping to continue for a time to operate under a continuous measure of public supervision of some kind.

I want here to insert a word about the position of those industries and businesses which are not within

the general field I have been considering. While it is
true that combination in its various forms has been
rapidly spreading in our country, and that it now ob-
tains in many of the most powerful and important of
our industries and businesses, it is also true that in
terms of individual numbers there are far more independent firms and businesses than there are fully
organised ones. I am thinking of the medium-sized and
small manufacturing businesses in all its great numbers. The small engineering shop, the garage, the
individual retail shop in its hundreds of thousands.
These units lie outside the territory with which I have
dealt. They are representatives of the tradition of
private enterprise; they do take risks; indeed many of
them have a very hard time and win their successes by
good hard thinking and hard work. Most businesses
of this kind do pay a real social dividend. They earn
their independence. So far from advocating public
interference with enterprises of this type (an enormous
task in any case which we could not attempt so long
as the problems of the larger firms and the organised
industry are with us), I am thinking of the rights and
the freedoms of these lesser firms as one of the reasons
why we ought to give public policy a large say in the
conduct of the rest. It would be a savage piece of
political irony and a reflection on the common sense
of all these medium-sized and small business people
if they allowed themselves to be led astray by tirades
about Government interference inspired by the bigger
interests whose freedom from public control would in
fact be a menace to the smaller ones. The medium and
small manufacturing business may well be in the
hands of some great monopoly firm or cartel for the

supply of many of its important raw materials. Many shopkeepers are either in the hands of wholesalers or dependent upon wholesalers who are themselves members of some fairly close commercial ring. The more the public interest and the interest of consumers represented by the State is imposed upon these large bodies, the better for the smaller people.

This will make it clear that in one way and another I am forced to the conclusion that there will be, and in a sense ought to be, a good deal of business activity carried on among us without State operation or control.

Does it then follow that this area of comparatively free individualistic enterprise is likely to become a breeding ground for that economic insecurity and periodic depression which has been our curse in the past? I am not unduly pessimistic about this.

All this of course implies an attitude on the part of the State towards the economic life of the counry far more positive and constructive than we have ever known. The State must in fact have a comprehensive economic policy. And that policy must be based upon a comprehensive knowledge of economic fact and circumstance to which we have begun to make some approach in recent years but of which in its full, necessary form we still fall short. There must be available to the Government a full and complete picture of the national economy and its prospects, the over-all relation between the different forms of earnings within it, the relation between the different forms of earnings within it, the relation between that part of the product of industry which is distributed as dividend, that part which is allotted to research, capital re-equipment

and technical improvement and that part which is put
to general reserve. The State must possess and act
upon a moving blueprint of the community's productive organisation. Where it does not operate it or
control it, it must at least understand it and the factors
and tendencies that work it. By this means it can use
its own power to regulate where it does not own or
operate. Thus it can achieve stability and assist the
long-term expansion which is the basis of full employment.

It is only fair to remember that some of the unfor-
tunate accompaniments of combination and association
in our industry in the past have been the result, not
so much of the combination, but of the world depression and shrinkage of markets which indeed the
combination often arose to counter. The Governments
of the world and our own Government at home will,
I hope and trust, try to frame policies that will set the
world firmly in the path of a long-term steady process
of economic expansion. They will try to clear away
the minefields of currency difficulties, world restrictive arrangements, trade barriers, depression in the
primary producing areas, and so forth. If they suc-
ceed, we shall have taken a great step for the en-
couragement on the part of many industrial associations and groups of a policy more in line with public
well-being than were the policies which they adopted,
or which were imposed upon them, before the war.
When an expanding market can be forseen, when it is
reasonable to hope that the shadow of recurrent
slumps can be exorcised by new methods. in finance
and industry, the restrictive mind of some of the pre-
war associations may give place to an expansive mind,

tending to seek its own good in greater sales to wider markets on the basis of increasing productivity and lower costs. I am not expressing any strong confidence in this outcome, I only say that unless we can achieve the conditions in which it becomes possible, then the world society is most certainly heading for another catastrophe.

Now lastly, I have just referred to high productivity and low cost as the essential basis of a healthy new regime from the side of industry. I would emphasise again the fundamental importance of this point. We must face the fact that some of our greatest and most vital industries have an efficiency strongly reminiscent of the curate's egg. They are very uneven. The high quality of the best part of them is the strongest and most convincing condemnation of the backwardness of the worst. This is a thing the nation cannot afford to tolerate. By replanning, by mechanisation, by rationalisation, by technical education of the workers, and by every measure that governments can adopt to help, it is essential that our industries be made over and put in a position of ability to compete with the best the world can show. I have sometimes detected among utterances on this questions a certain readiness to assume that because of difference in size or natural opportunity we must in some spheres accept a position of permanent inferiority to America and admit levels of casts and prices permanently above hers. This is where the old dragon of restrictionism and defeatism is seen raising his head—the poisonous creature that did so much to lay waste the national spirit of the national life before the war. I do not believe there is any obstacle standing between our great industries and a top-line level of supreme efficiency, except the belief of some of our industrialists themselves that is expecting too much. The whole of our approach to the problem of the State's relation to industry after the war must be animated by a determination to have done with this attitude. There is a great future for British workers and British industry. What is wanted is a change of methods and of heart.

TOWARDS INDUSTRIAL DEMOCRACY

By T. W. AGAR

B EFORE we answer the question as to whether the developments in war-time industry have taken us any measurable distance along the road towards industrial democracy, we must first of all get quite clear in our minds what we mean by democracy in industry. As far as I am concerned, I must say at once that I do not believe industrial democracy is possible until industry is publicly owned. Surely industrial democracy presupposes political democracy and economic freedom. You can tell a worker that he enjoys the benefits of democracy because he is allowed to vote for whom he pleases; that is one thing: it is another if he can be sacked five minutes afterwards by his employers. Political democracy under capitalism is one thing, functional democracy is another.

During the transition period from capitalism to socialism, there can be no such thing as an all-inclusive democracy. There can be no democracy, much less industrial democracy, while class divisions exist. There can be no real industrial democracy between those who dominate society and those who are its wage slaves, and the political objective of the Labour movement should be the bringing into existence of a much broader and more highly developed form of democracy, both political and functional.

Let us thoroughly understand, then, that real industrial democracy involves the complete disappearance of private ownership from industry. *Industrial democracy involves the control of industry by the workers engaged in it, and this means all workers, managerial, supervisory, scientific and technical, manual and operative,* answerable only to a higher economic general staff which in turn is subject to the Government as a whole. The measure of industrial democracy which the workers have gained during the war reflects the degree of political democracy which we have achieved. No more and no less.

Is it true that the power of monopolies has been curbed during the war? Is it true that the workers have gained any measure of real control? In both cases the answer is an emphatic no. It is true that the introduction of Joint Production Committees in the factories has given the workers a certain amount of say in the workshop. It is true that under the Essential Work Order an employer cannot sack a worker without giving good reasons for it. He must seek the permission of the National Service Officer. It is equally true that hundreds of workers have been sacked, their crime being trade union activity, and it is not very difficult for any empoylers to find a pretext.

In theory the Essential Work Order is designed to operate with fairness to both sides, but in practice only the workers are penalised. Time and again unions affiliated to the Trades Union Congress have raised their voices in strong protest at the continued acquiescence on the part of the Ministry of Labour and National Service in the imprisonment and punishment of boys and girls, men and women, for breaches of the Act, whilst it appears as though employers may flout it at will.

In my own union I have had to deal with the cases of members, highly skilled and technically trained, who have been dismissed on the grounds of redundancy when their real " crime " was the fact that they were doing their best to introduce new methods and planning into their shops with a view to increasing production. An increasing number of anti-trade union employers are using this argument that redundancy exists, when in fact it does not, and it is a very difficult thing for any union representative to argue before an Appeal Board that redundancy does not exist, when the higher management has access to all the facts and can cook up any case. In one of these cases we won the appeal and the National Service Officer directed our number back to work. Despite this the higher management refused him admittance to the factory, thus defying the Order. We discovered that so long as the firm paid his wages they need not reinstate him.

In October an eighteen-year-old girl was given six months' imprisonment for being late. At a certain missed for putting union letters on the notice board London firm a convenor of shop stewards was disat the factory. He appealed and won, but the firm refused to re-engage him. They are, however, paying his wages whilst he walks about doing nothing.. The Hendon Trades Council is conducting a campaign against the firm. Such happenings can be multiplied by the hundred. God knows how much time and skill have been lost to the nation because of such reactionary employers. Is there any industrial democracy here?

We also have experience where the Chairman of Local Appeal Boards have refused to allow evidence to be given by the workers' representatives, whilst employers are given every facility to make the most of their case. I know that I voice the opinions of most responsible trade union leaders when I say that whilst there are some good points in the Act, in the main it is generally looked upon as pro-employer and anti-worker.

Why is it that the National Arbitration Tribunal is so suspect? No union will go to the Tribunal unless it is forced to do so, for experience has proved that no matter how good your case, there exists a feeling that the Tribunal is determined to keep wages down. Out of five members there is only one workers' representative, whilst the Chairman are, of course, neutral. That is to say, neutral as far as their whole background will allow them to be. Is neutrality conditioned? A Chairman of the National Arbitration Tribunal, coming from the legal profession and having attained eminence in that profession, must find it difficult to judge a case impartially. Does his whole environment and background (I say it with all respect) permit him to see the workers' point of view? In a society of employers and workers I, for one, consider it next door to impossible to provide a really independent chairman.

The machinery agreed upon between the Government, the Employers' Federation and the Trades Union Congress to obtain the maximum war effort undoubtedly provides for representation of the men's trade unions locally, in the · district, and nationally. It is quite true that the voice of the worker may be heard on every Advisory Board and Committee which has been set up. Here I use the term "worker" in · its operative and manual sense, for the trades unions representing the technical, scientific and supervisory workers have no representation.

This is due to the fact that the unions catering for this type of professional worker are still unrecognised by the various employers' federations...The key men in British industry are the technicians, the planning engineers, the scientists and the supervisory workers. Is it not a ridiculous state of affairs that after four years of war they are not allowed representation on any advisory committee simply because the employers refuse to recognise their trade unions?

It will be seen how much industrial democracy these key people have been able..to obtain when their right to be represented by a *bona-fied* trade union is denied by the employers. Appeals to the various Ministries fall upon deaf ears, for it is obvious that the business men at the head of the various departments at the Ministry of Supply, who are the real controllers, are not likely to use their great powers for the benefit of trade unionism. For example, Sir Andrew Duncan, the Minister of Supply is President of the British Iron and Steel Federation, and the Iron and Steel Federation is a bitter enemy of trade unionism for technical, scientific and supervisory staffs. This is an aspect of the danger of industrialists in control at the various Ministries which has not yet been touched upto.

To return to the manual and operative workers for a moment, I think it can be said that out of their experiences, gained during service on the great network of Joint Production Committees, Joint Consultative Committees and all the other   Advisory Committees which have been set up during the war, has come some little knowledge of managerial functions, and this should prove very useful in the future.

This brings me to the vital questions of managerial functions, still regarded as the sole preserve of employers. This is a question which the trade union movement has neglected far too long. Our movement needs to get rid of its inferiority complex, for it is a fact that on the whole the trade union movement takes the view that managerial functions are the property, sacred and inviolated, of the owners of industry. At the 1942 Trades Union Congress a resolution was carried, demanding that the workers be given a share in management. There was, however, a bitter opposition by some of the larger general workers' unions, and a very big vote was cast against it.

If the industrial arm of the movement is ever to fulfil its historic mission, it must consider the problem of management as possibly the most pressing question facing it. It is all very well for prominent Labour Ministers to advocate the destruction of the vast concentrations of economic power wielded by trusts and cartels. We all agree with this, but I at least am concerned at the fact that all their speeches would have us believe that the moment the war ceases, we shall enter a transition period to socialism in one form or another. I think they take far too much for granted. I do not believe it will be so easy. I do not believe for one minute that the vested interests at present holding back the Scott, Uthwatt and Beveridge Reports are likely to give way without a terrific struggle on any of the major issues.

I do not want to see, indeed I am apprehensive at the prospect of seeing, the trusts and cartels as they at present exist being replaced by State trusts, increasingly multiplied by legislation without the introduction of safeguards designed to maintain genuine popular control over them. God help the trade unions if they have to negotiate with a multiplicity of public corporations on the conditions of service of the workers engaged therein. One does not solve the problem by appointing to the higher executive a well-known trade unionist. The problem was certainly not solved in this way in the case of the London Passenger Transport Board.

The terms of reference of this speech are limited, and I have not the opportunity of developing the question of the function of a House of Industry to which I shall refer, but it may well be that the possibilities of an "Industrial Parliament", answerable only to a universally elected House of Commons, would be at least one guarantee against what might easily become a corporate state instead of a workers' state.

I am not one of those people who would be disappointed if the capitalist interests did not put up a fight to retain their privileges and power, and for this reason in my opinion great tasks face the movement, political and industrial, if we are to prepare ourselves and provide the movement with an efficient machine really capable of running industry if we are ever called upon to do so.

If, by some unforeseen chance, the Labour movement were given the power in its hands to introduce as full a measure of socialism as possible, could we truthfully say that we were ready? Have we a machine, ready prepared to take industry over when we are mandated to run it, from which all vested interests have been eliminated? Are the two twings of our movement sufficiently dovetailed so as to ensure that the complicated problems of socialist construction could be tackled immediately? The honest answer is no. Political decisions may be one thing, industrial implementation is another.

Have we sufficient men of experience, imbued with socialist enthusiasm and loyalty, and possessing the essential managerial and technical qualifications to rely upon ? In the early transition period I visualise many problems and much opposition from those elements which would be prepared to adopt any tactics to upset socialist construction. Such a time will be extremely dangerous, and the movement will indeed have to adopt the slogan " Eternal vigilance is the price of liberty ", and in these circumstances the industrial movement should come into its own.

In so far as the trade union movement itself is concerned, the time is long overdue for a declaration of policy as to the role of the trade unions within a socialist state. There are many schools of thought on this question, but before it is able to tackle the problem of workers' control of industry in one form or another, it must needs first put its own house in order.

We lack vision : we think in terms of the wage system and minor reforms achieved by collective bargaining within the framework of capitalism. We do not see ourselves as a house of industry. We do not see ourselves as a parliament of workers, the function of which is the running of industry. We accept the wage system as a permanent phenomenon, and too much of the time of the movement is occupied in a selfish scramble for membership and in other inter-union disagreements. The vitally important question of function has, been totally disregarded. The General Council of the Trades Union Congress should be representative of function and not of numerical membership. There can be no doubt that the complete reorganisation of the trade unions along the lines of industrial unionism or organisation by industry would be a big step forward. The scientific, technical and supervisory workers must be organised horizantally, whilst operative and manual workers must be organised in their appropriate trade unions, industry by industry.

The trade unions are democratic institutions within the framework of capitalism, but they are certainly not capitalist democratic institutions ; they were not established by the capitalists but by the workers, and their functions would be greatly developed under a new economic system. This new economic system must not mean the extension of corporations like the London Passenger Transport Board, for although this has been described by some of the political leaders of our movement as a measure of socialism, any trade union official who has dealings with the Board will tell you that dealing with the Board's executive is no different from dealing with the directors of any capitalist concern.

It is the job of the trade unions to take this question of management very seriously. It has been said that planning and managemet of production will be a crucial test for a socialist society and must be of the highest quality. The trade union movement must commence to train the managers of the future, and it must seek to bring to its ranks an ever-increasing number of managers who are disgusted with the waste and corruption of capitalist society. There is no reason why the Trades Union Congress should not set up its own college to take on this important task.

A manager needs two qualities : (*a*) the ability to plan, and (*b*) the ability to lead. Leadership in industry is not simply a matter of exercising authority based upon the power of the sack. The manager of the future must exercise his authority by virtue of personal example. My own union is engaged at the moment in hammering out a code of conduct for managers. Our movement has constantly neglected the role of manager. There is far too much confusion between management and ownership.

In his excellent Fabian pamphlet, " Management in Transition," Austen Albu says that training for management, as indeed the whole subject of training for industry, is one which needs a great deal of investigation and co-ordination, and that it cannot be considered apart from the general education programme of the country. In the U.S.S.R. selected technicians with a flair for leadership are sent to industrial academies, where they receive specialised training.

Until either the state or industry itself demands a standard of knowledge an experience from those who aim at managerial positions, the situation is unlikely to develop very fast and industry will muddle along with great variations in the organisations of its different units. Albu says : " Under an economy with a large socialist planned content, it may be possible to make the manager in the private firm responsible to the State ; the precedent has been set in the new coalmins scheme. Failing that, there should be much greater statutory control of managerial actions. It might be a good rule that every undertaking over a certain size must have a qualified manager without financial interest in the firm.

" If managers have failed to organise professionally they have equally failed to organise for the maintenance of their rights and working conditions and for the presentation of their social and economic demands. Every attempt to organise managerial grades into unions or similar bodies has failed, but at last a *bonafide* trade union affiliated to the T.U.C. is endeavouring to awaken managers to their responsibilities within society and society to the importance of the quality of the managers, it gets."

The dire need for maximum production in this engineers' war threw into sharp relief the whole question of management. In scores of undertakings of all kinds, the workers accused their superiors of inefficient management, and in many cases they were dismissed as a direct result of the pressure brought to bear upon the various Ministries by the trade unions. These people found themselves without protection of any

kind. They had no organisation to turn to which'
could act as their counsel during the enquiry—their
Directors were not concerned, for there were plenty
of available managers to choose from, whilst the workers, whose whole industrial background compels them
to view the managers with hostility, were gleeful that
they had the opportunity of a long-awaited " kick
back ".

Some time ago we were asked by the men's unions
to support their efforts to secure the dismissal of a
works manager who was in their opinion hopelessly
inefficient. An enquiry resulted, and the manager
was dismissed. During the hearing, however, he
hotly contested all the evidence produced by the men's
unions and supported by the foremen and technicians.

He was removed ; and months afterwards that
manager came to my office to seek admission into that
branch of my union which caters only for managers.
He informed me that if he had had protection such as
my union could have afforded him during the enquiry,
he would have divulged many things which would
have removed the blame from his shoulders and
placed it squarely upon those of his superiors, i.e. the
directors. He saved their faces, and in doing so, fell
between two stools.

Managers, like any other section of workers, salaried
or otherwise, need sound trade--union protection, and
it is high time they developed a professional complex
like the doctor, the lawyer and other professional
workers. Managers must develop a social conscious-
ness and sense of loyalty to the State.

Business brains and functional brains are fundamentally different. Business brains are in essence

devoted to the pursuit of profits and the maintenance of financial control without which they would immediately be submerged by brains moved purely by functional considerations. This distinction between business and functional brains has yet to be grasped by the leaders of our movement. They have never understood it, and yet it is one of the most, possibly the most vital problem facing us. It may be that we could do worse than copy with the necessary adaptations the structure of the trade union movement as it exists in the Soviet Union. That is one school of thought.

It may be that we could do worse than abolish the House of Lords and substitute for it the House of Industry, but whatever we do it is absolutely essential that our political leaders pay far more attention to the whole of the trade union movement in the transition period to socialism that they have done or are doing at present. The trade union movement may have some shortcomings, but our political leaders must be given to understand that the trade unions cannot be expected to view with favour and with joyful anticipation the prospects of their being dictated to by permanent civil servants with little or no knowledge of industrial functionalism. I am no syndicalist. I am well aware that industry must function within the nation's economy as a whole and that at all times it would have its responsibilities.

Nationalisation of industry is meaningless without some measure of workers' control. Political power in Westminster must be correlated to industrial power exercised by the workers, professional and manual, through their unions. Even our labour-controlled councils are terribly backward on this vital question and create confusion and dismay in the minds of their employees by their complete lack of co-operation with the trade unions.

Why should not the London County Council call the various unions catering for hospital employees into consultation when it proposes reorganisation ? Apart from the practical experience based upon first-hand knowledge that these people could give to their political colleagues holding the power, it would create in the workers a new self-confidence. If the leaders of the London County Council were asked the reason for this, they would undoubtedly reply that they are responsible for their stewardship to the ratepayers and not to the Labour movement. In my opinion this is a weakness, and we shall have to decide whether or not a parliamentary majority in the House must primarily be responsible to the nation or to the Labour movement for its stewardship.

There is a danger of our movement falling between two stools because of its lack of confidence in the common people. The surest way to remedy this grievance is to ensure that on all questions of reorganisation and economic planning, the trade unions shall be looked upon as equal partners.

The trade unions must face the fact that power will bring grave functional responsibilities. At present there is insufficient understanding between the political and industrial arms of our movement. Indeed, there is friction. There are many people in the T.U.C. and its affiliated unions who have learned by painful experiece that labour people in high office seldom use that office for the benefit of the trade unions. This friction must be stopped if we are to get anywhere.

I believe that to say we have achieved any real industrial democracy during the war would be to indulge in wishful thinking. Now the threat to the British Empire has receded into the background I believe that—mainly by reason of the Russian victories—the vested interests in this country are showing their teeth more and more (and they are not false teeth) and with every day that passes the British trade union movement is losing its bargaining strength.

Employers of all kinds are guilty of actions to-day which they dare not have dreamed of at the time of Denkirk. I hate to be a pessimist, for I have to be a super-optimist in my own job, but I am bound to admit that in so far as real industrial democracy is concerned, very little has been achieved during the war. There is a growing mass of black-coated workers, scientists, architects and technicians, not forgetting managers, who have at last begun to understand their identity of interest with all other sections of workers, both by hand and brain. This in itself is a revolution, and it took this ghastly war to achieve it. It is an indispensable step in the direction of socialist society. The Marxians would call it a dialectical change, but whatever we call it, it is a phenomenon the nature of which the industrial movement has yet fully to understand, and, having understood it, canalise it to the desired ends.

FREEDOM UNDER PLANNING

by BARBARA WOOTTON

I AM conscious that in the title chosen for this lecture there is only one word which is precise in meaning and emotionally unbiased : that is the middle word " under ". I shall, therefore, have to begin by asking you not, indeed to spend much time on definitions, but at least to get a moderately clear notion of what both freedom and planning mean in practical life. I am not going to philosophise over elaborate defiitions of freedom. There are plenty such ; indeed seldom, perhaps, have such fine hairs been split by so many to so little purpose as in the making of philosophical definitions. I am going to ask you to agree with me that for all practical purposes this afternoon we know fairly well what freedom means.

We recognise freedom, if in no other way, by its opposite. We know very well the peculiar emotion, the frustration, which accompanies loss of freedom. Perhaps as good a working definition of freedom as we can find is that, where there is no frustration, there there is freedom. At the same time, we recognise as a fact that complete absence of frustration is not possible ; for complete liberty for any one individual is possible only for that one individual. Absolute liberty implies omnipotence ; and the world cannot contain more than one omnipotent person. Hence, following Burke, we must admit that " freedom must be limited to be possessed ". So much for freedom.

Now for planning. This word has acquired in recent years, amongst the political " Left ", a flavour of approbation. To plan is, by presumption, to plan well and wisely. This is perhaps a little odd, because of all the plans that have been made in the world throughout recorded history, I should have thought at least as many would incur our condemnation as would win our appproval. Nevertheless, planning has come to stand for something that you and I want. Since, however, it is possible to plan for evil as well as for good, we ought to be clear about the essential meaning of planning in our particular context.

For this afternoon, planning means economic planning, and economic planning means a conscious and deliberate choice by representatives of the community of the use to which our economic resources shall be put. That may, on the face of it, sound a little vague ; but it can quite easily be reduced to more precise and concrete terms. It means that the major economic decisions, such as—Shall we grow our own food ? What shall be spent on education ? How much income shall you have, and how much shall be my share ? To what extent shall we keep alive industries which are superseded by new techniques ? What kind of work shall we do ?—it means that the major economic decisions of this kind are made *deliberately* by someone acting on behalf of all the people concerned. And I would add that it is not planning in the full sense, unless the people who make those decisions are clothed with the majesty of the State : that is to say, unless they have behind them the legal force which the State alone enjoys.

Before we pass to the relation between freedom and

planning, we had better perhaps notice that planning in this sense is not quite identical with nineteenth-century Socialism. Nor, for that matter, is the twentieth-century Fabian Society identified with nineteenth-century Socialism. Planning in this sense does not necessarily ivolve the public ownership of the means of production, distribution, and exchange. Planning may, in practice, be combined with 100 per cent. public ownership ; or it may in practice, be found to lead irresistibly towards public ownershp : but planning and Socialism are not the same thing. What planning does involve is what has sometimes been called the socialisation of demand, i.e. the determination by a public authority of what is to be produced and where—which is not the same thing as a decision by that authority to undertake the production itself. That distinction becomes clear if we look at the present world. In time of war we do not have Socialism in the sense of the national ownership of the whole productive machine, but we do have the socialisation of demand over a very wide field. The Government settle what is to be made, even if they do not themselves always make it, but, instead place their orders with private enterprise.

Now there are two pictures of a planned society which are familiar to us all. It was, I think, Bertrand Russell who said that, if the temperature of a room should unhappily become the subject of political controversy, there would be two parties : the one would advocate that the temperature should be freezing, and the other that it should be at boiling-point. Something of that kind may be said about these two pictures of freedom and planning. In the first picture,

planning and freedom march happily together. Indeed, in the extreme forms of this picture, not only
do they march happily together ; they are actually
bound in indissoluble wedlock. Those who imagine
a Socialist society in these colours not only see no
contradiction between freedom and planning ; they
presume a logical and necessary connection between
the two, and assume that where there is planning,
there there is freedom.

That is one picture. I think that that is the picture
we know best. I am not going to say a great deal
about it, because one may take for granted, amongst
Fabians, that is familiar enough. Indeed, it is just
because planning is so widely believed to be the
straight road to freedom that " to plan " has come to
have the agreeable implications of which I spoke just
now.

The second picture is the exact opposite. In this,
freedom and planning are by no means bound in eternal union. They are in bitter and deadly enmity, and
the more you plan the less you are free. As the
grasping hand of the planner extends, so the cowed
and harried citizen shrinks into an ever narrower
circle of liberty. If the first is the picture drawn by
the Fabian Society on the left, the second, on my
right, is the picture that haunts the school of Sir
Ernest Benn.

Let us look at these two pictures a little more con-
cretely and realistically. The first commends itself
very easily, because any person who walks about the
streets of this or any other city knows that without
security there is no freedom. No one who does not
know where his next meal is coming from is free to

do anything except make sure of that meal. That is the first truth illustrated in this picture. The second truth is equally plainly established by experience. Security is not a thing that happens of itself. Security is not realised unless it is planned. Therefore you say with confidence, appealing to experience, that since freedom depends on security, and security depends on planning, it follows that where there is no planning, there cannot be freedom.

What, however, we cannot assert with equal confidence is the converse of that proposition. It may well be true that where there is no planning, there there is no freedom : and at the same time it may equally be *un*true that where there is planning, there there is necessarily freedom.

At this stage we have to make a number of distinctions. The first is a distinction between those freedoms which are affected by *any* kind of planning, whether for better or for worse, and those which might be threatened only by planning far worse. To put it another way, we have to consider both how far freedom is affected by the *fact* of planning, and how far is it only affected by the *content* of the plans and the *method* of planning. That distinction is fundamental to the whole discussion. Failure to appreciate it has led people to denounce planning *as such* in terms which are appropriate only to bad planning, and equally to applaud planning in terms appropriate only to good plans. We have got to be clear both about the implications of planning itself, and about the other issues that are contingent upon the actual content and purpose of any particular plan.

Let us consider first the fact of planning, that is,

the effects upon freedom of *any kind* of planning. For that purpose we will shelve the second part of the problem, and make an easy step of the imagination. We will assume that our plan is made by people as nice, as public-spirited, and as immune from the love of power as ourselves—an assumption which is practically always made by planners.

Now the freedoms that most people care about are concrete. They may be classfied as civil, as economic, and as political ; and I want to say straight away that I can see no conceivable connection between economic planning and what are generally called the civil freedoms. There is no rational cause to expect that established civil freedoms should be afforded, certainly not for the worse and probably not for the better either, by economic planning. By civil freedoms I mean the right to speak disrespectfully of persons in high places : I mean rights of public meeting : I mean a large number of legal and judicial rights, which in this country we cherish very highly in theory, and to some extent respect in practice. It is often said that in a planned society you will not be able to open your mouth. You will be liable to be removed at dead of night and imprisoned without trial, and so on. Those fears are groundless ; for there is no logical connection whatever between a State decision to determine the output of agriculture or of mining, and not being able to open your mouth.

It is a concidence, I think a very unhappy coincidence, but still a coincidence, that the only large experiment in economic planning that we have seen has been in a community where the civil freedoms that the British value so highly have never existed. That makes it easy for people who have observed that, in Soviet Russia, economic planning is *not* combined with civil freedoms on the British model, to suggest that these freedoms, which we so rightly prize, are necessarily threatened by economic planning. It would be just as logical to argue that the dry climate of California is derived from the tariffs imposed by the United States Federal Government, as to suggest that the absence of civil freedoms in the U.S.S.R. is *due* to economic planning. In each case two things co-exist in the same place but there is no logical connection between them. So far as the civil freedoms are concerned they are indeed immensely important. Let him think twice who belittles them. But they have nothing to do with economic planning. They can be ripened and safeguarded where there is economic security, but they are not threatened by the fact of planning.

Now let us turn to the economic freedoms. The primary economic freedom we have already mentioned ; it is that freedom from haunting insecurity which enables one to avail oneself of all other freedoms. I do not need to elaborate on that. The primary economic freedom can only be guaranteed ,by planning because, as I said earlier, it does not happen of itself. It is untrue that men are born free ; and no less untrue, at any rate, that women are born free. They are made free by deliberate and conscious regulation. Nevertheless, there may yet be some economic freedoms which are not so obviously in harmony with economic planning.

Our main economic freedoms, other than those of which I have spoken, are freedom with limits to choose what work we will do ; freedom, within limits, to choose how we will spend the reward that we get for that work; and freedom, within limits, to influence the amount of the reward that we get.

So far as the first two of these freedoms are concerned, I think a common principle runs through any economic plan. First of all, we have to be honest about it. It is no good making a plan if you do not provide the means of carrying it out. It is no good writing your plans down in a big book with 40,000 pages—I think that was the length of the first Russian plan—if nothing ever gets outside the covers of that book. It is no good deciding what the output of coal, or of foodstuffs, or of pots and pans and boots and shoes is to be, if effective steps are not taken to see that those outputs are in fact realised.

Equally, it is no good planning consumption if people will not, or do not, consume the things which you in your wisdom have provided for them. It is no good planning that they should have opportunities of strength through joy, if they prefer joy through weakness. Planning, in fact, does imply that in practice we must get the answers right, and that somehow people must do the things which the planners have planned that they shall do.

Now here enters our common principle, in the form of a choice that is open to us. First, one way of getting people to carry out our plans is by direct order. That, at least, is effective. We know that only too well from experience. It is, however, desirable in this connection to call a spade a spade (certainly to call an order an order), so as to make the choice with our eyes open. We must revise our vocabulary, and stop saying "direction", when we mean conscription. Direct order, that is to say industrial conscription, is one way of deciding who is to work at what in a planned economy.

I am not going to say very much about that. You are in a good position, either at first or at second hand, to judge whether you like that method or not. I only ask you to think very seriously, especially those of you who are still yourselves undirected, of the responsibility of imposing what is called direction, and is in fact compulsion, on others permanently. I do not mind telling you that I do not myself like it. I do not like people to be ordered into and out of jobs even for the best of reasons by the best of authorities. But happily this course is not necessary, because we have the choice of an alternative way.

The alternative is to get people to do the work you have planned that they should do, not by direct order on individuals, but by so arranging the conditions and attractions of the work that a suitable number of people voluntarily choose to do it ; out of the range of opportunity open to them, enough people prefer the particular jobs that the plan needs done. Planning by alternatives to planning by direct compulsion ; and it is, I think, very interesting that in the Soviet Union the policy until the war—and war circumstances, as you know, are special—has been steadily towards planning by inducement, and away from planning by compulsion. Inducement covers no end or things, and you can amuse yourselves very profitably by turning over in your minds the particular inducements that would make you take up particular jobs where there may be a shortage of labour. Some may be financial ;

some may not. There is a very wide range of motives to which the State can appeal, beginning with public spirit—it has to be put first, even if it is not the most powerful—and ending with financial advantages.

The same choice runs through planning for consumption. Again, we have to recognise that what we produce, that and nothing else shall we consume; and that it is stupid to make a plan for providing all kinds of fancy goods, if those goods are not what are wanted. Again, planning for consumption *can*, within limits, be carried out by direct order; but the limits are narrower than in the planning of people's work. And, again, inducement is the alternative to compulsion.

Now there are not many things that you can compel people to consume. Education is the most conspicuous. But even there it may be disputed whether, in fact, you can force anyone to consume education. You can compel people to consume time in a particular building for a particular number of hours, but that is not necessarily the same thing as consuming education. Moreover, anybody who has fed a reluctant child knows that even to enforce the consumption of a desirable food like milk is not an entirely easy job. Therefore, planning for consumption, thanks to the nature of things, is less easily achieved by direct compulsion than is the planning of production.

It has, indeed, been suggested that in a planned economy we might have no choice as to what we were allowed to consume..no choice, in fact, either as to the work that we should do, or as to what we should get for that work. Well we might not; but let me repeat, this result is not *necessary*. There is no reason why we should all wear a standard uniform in the planned economy of peace time. The Russians didn't. There is no reason why we should even have a standard education. It is possible to plan for variety, and for that variety to give choice. The essential condition is that what is produced should be so priced in relation to our incomes that we are able to make a real choice from what is available. In an economically planned society, you do not necessarily have to eat. and dress like everybody else or go without. You have your money and your points in your pocket,. and you make your choice. The difference between this and a market economy is, first, that your choice does not necessarily regulate what is going to be produced later; and, second, that the goods that are offered to you are deliberately priced at a figure which, if they are held to be essential, is within everybody's means.

Planning and individual consumer's choice (within the limits of what is produced, are thus quite compatible. The fact that the output of cigarettes and the output of sweets may be planned will not prevent a non-smoker from buying twice as many sweets as his neighbour who economises on toffee in order to be sure of a smoke. There may be some things that ought to be distributed in kind and without charge to everybody alike; but, in general, choice and variety can and should remain.

I hope that in one field, anyhow, they certainly will remain. We are interested not only in freedom to choose the goods and services that we buy with the rewards of our labour, but also in freedom to choose what to do with the time when we are not working. It is greatly to be hoped that our economic planners will walk most warily when it comes to what is called the planning of leisure. It has been well said that the only problem of anyone's leisure is to prevent other people from using it.

Thus I suggest to you that right through both consumption and production there remain two roads to the same goal. The plan can be translated into action either by direct order : " You and you and you will do this and that and the other job " ; or it can be made effective by the use of appropriate attractions and incentives : " Here is the job. Which of you would like how many of them ? "

We come now to the somewhat more difficult questions connected with our freedom to influence the reward paid for our work ; that is, the right of bargaining in a planned economy. Here, too, we must be honest and realistic. If any group of people in a strong bargaining position (and for this purpose it makes no difference whether they are bargaining with a public authority or a private employer)—if any group of people in a strong bargaining position choose to exploit that position to the full without reference to the effects of their action on others, those people will wreck any plan. It is not possible, first, to plan that certain things shall be produced and sold at certain prices, and then to leave the payment made to those employed in the making and selling of them to be determined by the economic strength of the parties directly concerned. That we have to recognise. The practical social consequences of this situation will depend largely on the vision and good sense of the trade union movement.

Here, first, as our planning develops, we shall need,

I think, to train ourselves to look at the field of bargaining rather differently. The present range of trade union action (I do not speak of the war) is always sectional : each individual union, representing one section of the workers, presses, as and when it can, the claims of that one section to the full. There is no wage policy : there are as many distinct wage policies as there are separate unions. Under a general economic plan, with full employment, there is real danger that these policies may nullify one another. The gains of each group may be reflected in a rising cost of living, and thus lead to further claims from others who are injured by this rise. If this happens, we shall be spinning up the vicious spiral before we know where we are. Hence a first condition of economic planning (if the right of free bargainning is to remain) is that wage claims should be co-ordinated ; and that unions should refrain from putting forward claims for higher wages for any one group of workers, when these can only be satisfied at the expense of other workers in other trades or districts.

Second, the trade unions will have to extend their functions in another direction. They will be concerned not so much with getting five shillings extra for the railway workers, or ten shillings more for the miners ; but rather with raising the share of working as a whole in the national income, and of raising it in real things as well as in money. In a planned society the job of the unions is increasingly to improve the output and efficiency of industry, to keep *down* the price level quite as much as to keep *up* the level of money wages.

On this fundamental issue of the compatibility of

planning with free collective bargaining we cannot unfortunately learn much from the only large-scale economc planning that we know, because the Soviet trade unions do not in fact enjoy freedom of collective bargaining as we understand it here. They do not exercise the ultimate power collectively to withdraw their labour. Now we in Britain have that power, and I do not think that we are going lightly to give it away. But the mere fact that we have it is, of course, a *potential* threat to any plan. I am sure that the sensible thing to do is to retain that right in the hope that it will be sensibly exercised, and that, in practice, the trade unions will appreciate the incompatibility of sectional bargaining and successful planning.

There are some lessons to be learnt here from the war the moral of which is that we had better not be too logical. Thus I read, in the *Ministry of Labour Gazette* in June, 1940, an official notice that under the Emergency Powers Act, people who had not followed a certain procedure would render themselves liable to penalties if they should strike. The Order to that effect was long and impressive. But I notice also with interest that even from June, 1940, onwards, the same official Journal officially and publicly records month by month the number of strikes that have taken place without any penalties apparently being imposed on anybody ! That is a charming piece of illogicality and one on which we might do well to build.

So now, it seems, we get to this. The *fact* of planning involves no risk at all to our civil freedoms ; it does raise problems about our economic freedoms ; but these *can* be solved without resort to compulsion, and without loss of liberties that we rightly value.

I come now to poiltical freedoms. Once more we must begin by facing the issue. It has often been said that you cannot have effective economic planning if there is more than one political party. And once more example is no comfort, for the only example that we have of comprehensive economic planning is a one-party State. Is the abolition of party politics necessary for economic planning ? I do not think it is. But those who hold a different opinion are, nevertheless, posing a real problem. For we cannot, by definition, make a continuous long term plan for, say, five years and still change our minds every six months. If the existence of political parties does mean the right to change our minds about *everything* every six months then I am afraid it is incompatible with long-term planning.

What is the moral of that ? Surely it is that you cannot have economic planning unless there are some things about which people are not going to change their minds. In other words, unless there is a common agreement throughout the community, roughly co-extensive with the aims of the plan, the plan will be ineffective. If there is no such agreement, and there are still political parties and free elctions, then it will sometimes happen that one party is elected in June and embarks on a five years' plan, and that this is promptly reversed when another party comes into power in December. Anybody who studies the history of housing policy in this country between the wars will appreciate the force of this. The schedule to the Act of 1924 provided a certain scale of subsidies payable over forty years. Two years later the rates of subsidy were substantially reduced. If that can happen, you cannot plan. In a divided community we shall have to walk rather carefully, to know where the boundaries of common agreement lie. Within those boundaries there will still be room for opposition parties, criticising, improving, and altering the plan at every stage ; but that opposition must accept, for the duration of the plan, the fundamentals which the plan is seeking to achieve. If we have that common agreement, then the necessary constitutional devices to give effect to it could very easily be invented. I am not a constitutional lawyer, and I would not like to say too much about the practical steps to be taken. But we could give some kinds of law, those which embody the main objectives of a plan, a more permanent status than others ; or we could establish public boards and corporations (on the B.B.C. or London Transport mode) and give them a definite long-term job to do. If a public corporation of that kind had been responsible for housing between the wars, the story might have been very different.

Now, in conclusion, I must ask you to abandon the romantic illusion that we have so far maintained—the illusion that every plan is by definition a good plan. Illusion it certainly is. For on the one hand there is no certainty that all plans will be devised by nice public-spirited people like ourselves. Not at all. And, on the other hand, people like ourselves are often much less nice and much less public-spirited when we get a little power into our hands. Some of the most serious problems of planning are concerned, not with the consequences of the fact of planning, but with the choice of the planners and the operation of the plan.

Here I can only open up a field which will be far

too wide for me to cover at all adequately. Let us
first remind ourselves that we have had a piece of
shocking bad luck in the last three or four generations.
At the time when we came to think that democracy
was the right kind of government, there also happened—and this was the bad luck—other changes which
made democratic government particularly difficult.
Everybody knows that democracy works beautifully
in a group of half-a-dozen people who need to make
a decision on something that they all know a good
deal about. Everybody also knows that this is not
typical of political democracy. But just at the time
when democratic government began to be generally
accepted, the scale of the problems with which government has to deal became enormously enlarged.
That means that the infant democracy has had to
struggle with an exceptionally difficult job almost
beyond its little weakly powers. The most critical of
all the social problems of our time is this business
of combining large-scale government with democratic
government. I can only throw out one or two suggestions as to the lines on which the answer may
eventually be found.

First, I believe that we shall eventually have to
make the choice of our rulers less in terms of programmes, and more in terms of people and principles.
Large democracies (and they must be large) *cannot*
express accurate and informed opinions on the issues
which conscientious parliamentary candidates are
bound at present to submit to them. But we still can
form a pretty shrewd judgment as to who are the
people to be trusted and who are not. And we can
often sum up past records a good deal better than we

can judge between future promises and policies. Hence our job as electors will, I suggest, become more and more a matter of putting people into office for a term of years and letting them got on with it.

In the second place, we should encourage a shift of public political activity, as it wére, from the centre to the circumference. The individual elector should be less concernéd with major decisions of policy than with the constructive criticism of the day-to-day operation of policies that have already been adopted. At the fringe of every plan where it touches the individual, there should be a variety of local committees, democratically elected, criticising and assisting in the execution of the consumption plan criticising and assisting in the administration of food policy, of the social services, of the plan for recruitment of labour.

The labour of democracy for the ordinary citizen in service on local bodies of this kind ought to be an enormously wide one. I hope that we shall see the time when nearly every household has at least one member serving on some such active public body. Some of these committees will be advisory, like the committees now advising the Assistance Board ; some will be executive, ilke the present local Food Committees ; some judicial, like the Unemployment Courts of Referees.

The other and final suggestion is that the ultimate safeguard of freedom against the power-loving bureaucrat depends on what kind of people we are. You know the different sorts of people found in the world in which we already live. First we have those whose attitude towards any official regulation or document is one of helpless despair. There are thousands of people like that. I dare say most of us are like that. A paper has come about so and so. What do I have to do with it? "Oh, you sign here." There are still far too many people who "sign here". What do they sign? They sign the right for their case to be heard by two people instead of three. They sign a contract to pay so much a week for something the value of which they have never adequately considered. They sign away a right of appeal. They sign away all kinds of safeguards, which their representatives have carefully and deliberately devised for their protection. They sign those safeguards away because they are timid, ignorant, and helpless.

We know too many people like that. But we also occasionally meet citizens of another kind, and how formidable they are! I mean those who say right out, "I have a right to be considered innocent until I am proved guilty"; those who insist on calling a witness, even if it means that their case must be adjourned, and everybody concerned has to come back again next week; those who stick to it that "These are the grounds on which I claim exemption from fire-watching", and will not listen to irrelevancies.

I have met these stalwarts, and so have you; and I have sometimes thought how delightful it would be to live in a democracy in which everybody was like that. For in the end the guarantee of freedom is that we should *all* be intelligent, alert and informed, determined to discover our liberties and to demand them for ourselves and for others in particular cases, no less than in the large and fine-sounding terms of a general political programme.

How do you get a democracy like that? I do not

know any simple road to it ; but I think it is true that the creation of a society in which the average person is alert intelligent, informed and bursting with initiative —the creation of that kind of society is dependent upon profound social changes to which the whole programme of the Fabian Society is intended to contribute. It is dependent, for instance, on changes in education, in the distribution of wealth and in the distribution of both power and social prestige. But until everybody both can and will speak up for himself and his neighbour, freedom will always be insecure under the best plan as well as under the worst.

Let me, therefore, conclude by going back to Burke, with whom I began, and amending him. It is not only true that freedom must be limited to be possessed : freedom must also be used to be possessed.

CULTURE AND THE COMMUNITY

By C. E. M. JOAD

I expect I ought to begin by saying what I mean by culture. I am not going to give a clever definition. I know all sorts of clever definitions of cultivated persons, but I am not going to give you any of those, because I think we have had enough of clever people like ourselves laughing at ourselves. We have been doing it for the whole of the twenty-five years between the two wars, with the result that the community has been taking its cue from us and has been busy laughing at us ever since.

I will give you a serious one, such as you might have had in the Victorian age. I will say that a cultivated man is a man who cares for the things of the mind and the spirit ; who has good taste ; who believes that some things in art and literature are better than other things, and does· not merely mean by that that most people happen to like them ; who believes in his soul that Beethoven is better than Irving Berlin, even though most people at any time may happen to prefer Irving Berlin ; who is prepared to pursue, to make sacrifices for and zealously to adhere to the things that he believes to be beautiful, and is prepared so to discipline, train and use his mind that he may discover those things which are true.

All these things I mean by culture and by being a cultivated man. Now the first point to which I want to draw your attention—because it has a bearing on the place of culture in a socialist State—is the decline in the prestige of culture and the cultivated in our own age. The Victorians were brought up to love the highest when they saw it. We, on the contrary, are much more disposed to heave a brick at it. I am interested to analyse some of the reasons for that change.

As to the facts, I think there can be very little doubt. To be seen reading Wordsworth or Coleridge in public is a ground for shame. None of my acquaintances who care for poetry ever permit themselves to be seen reading poetry in the tube. If they do it, they do it privily and at night.

On the other hand, to be seen reading the *Daily Blank* or the *Picture Blanker* is a cause for congratulation. This is not only a statement of fact ; it is also an affirmation of values.

There is an essay somewhere by Aldous Huxley in a volume called *Music at Night*, in which he mentions the fact that Mr. Ernest Hemingway permits himself in one of his books to introduce the name of an Old Master—in a single phrase, no more, he refers to the bitter nail-holes in one of Mantegna's Christs. Then, appalled at his own temerity, he hastens on to speak once more of lower things. It is exactly, says Aldous Huxley, as if Mrs. Gaskell in one of her novels had been betrayed into speaking by inadvertence of a water-closet.

It seems to me that there are many results of this shame of culture. One of them is rather curious. It is that there is no background of general culture and general reading which can be taken for granted by educated persons of this generation.

When my generation was growing to maturity in the last period of our civilisation, just before 1914, there was a galaxy of great writers from whom one could choose one's readng. Behind us were the great Victorians ; contemporary were Shaw, Wells, Bennett, Belloc, Galsworthy and E. M. Forster, and just appearing above the horizon of the future, D. H. Lawrence, V. Woolf, A. Huxley, and others.

Naturally we had our favourites. I can remember at a College Debating Society speaking on what seemed to us then a proposition of overwhelming importance, " Whether Hardy or Meredith were the greater Novelist ", and I can remember—with shame now—that I spoke on the side of Meredith. There are no contemporary writers in the young man's library to-day to form an equivalent common, cultural background.

The point was brought home to me not so long ago—
it was in 1939—when I was talking to a young journal-
ist, alert and vigilant, keenly interested in affairs. I
asked him what he was reading. I was startled by his
ignorance into feeling the full burden of my age,
because it is only the middle aged who can be so
shocked by the young. It was not merely that he had
not read *Mr. Polly* and *Kipps*, that he had only vague-
ly heard of Shaw and did not know whether he was.
alive or dead ; that he had not heard of Yeats at all ;.
that when I lent him *The Idiot*, thinking he might care
to learn something of the great Russian novelists of
the nineteenth century, he could not. get through it.
In his literary firmament there were literally no stars
to take the places of the great men of the past. He
read Penguins, the productions of the Left Book Clubs,
encyclopaedias, anything which would give him the
sense of feeling and the appearance of being cultured
without the reality. It seems to me that this contemporary ignorance of culture was a new feature of our
civilisation, as it was just before the war.

I will give you two more examples, both of which
are post-war. I was interviewed by a young man who
was so good as to profess a desire to know my opinions
about broadcasting, as to which, indeed, I have many.
I am passionately fond of the music of Bach and.I
ventured to express the opinion that it would be a
good thing if more of such music were made available
to listeners or, more to the point, made available to
listeners at times when they could listen to it.

Rather to my surprise, practically all my opinions
appeared very much in the form in which I had expressed them. Only one had been excised, and that

was my favourable opinion of Bach. I asked the Editor for the reason. He replied to this effect: "Most of my readers are quite unable to distinguish between the music of Bach and the sound of water gurgling down a plug hole." I protested that Bach was a great man and an acknowledged master of music. "Surely," I said, "there cannot be any harm in making an offering on so conventional an altar." But I was told that my opinions were far from being conventional; that we live in an age of debunking; that it was not merely the case that people did not listen to Bach; more to the point was the fact that nobody now thought it necessary to take the trouble to pretend to like what they did not like—that, in other words, there was no longer a snobbery of culture.

I take one more example from the war itself. It affords a commentary upon the results of sixty or seventy years' popular education. I am in a train travelling from Edinburgh to London. It is packed with soldiers. It is an eight-hour journey, and the train is two or three hours overdue. The soldiers are standing packed in the corridors. They have long exhausted the rather slender resources of one another's conversation; have long ago plumbed the meagre delights of looking out of the window. There they sit or stand hour after hour in a misery of bored in-activity, and not to one in a hundred does it occur to read a book. Getting interested, I went through the train counting all ranks, officers as well as men, and I counted up to one hundred and four before I found the first soldier who was reading any book at all, and then it was *No Orchids for Miss Blandish*!

What a commentary on the results of seventy years

of popular education ! We have brought up a generation which has not the habit of reading, to whom it does not occur to read for pleasure, and to whom therefore the treasure house of the world's literature is closed.

Now a word or two on the causes of this situation. Here is the most important : that the highbrow, the intellectual, the cultivated man, is a bad consumer. He does not make any demands, or very little demands, upon the country's resources for the production of commodities, in order that he may live his life. Is he going about in a motor-car ? No. Is he whacking about little round bits of matter with long thin ones ? He is not. Is he hurling himself down the water chute at Southend, or on the switchback at Blackpool ? No. Sometimes he may be smoking, but that is about all he is doing and for the rest he is reading a book, probably price sixpence. If he is content with a green thought in a green shade, he is consuming nothing at all.

What a bad citizen ! All the resources of advertisement are being wasted upon him, and since the public taste and the public mind are very largely formed by advertisement, formed by those who produce and have something to sell, and since in the years before the war they were not able to sell all that they produced, a strong, unconscious sentiment of opprobrium was fomented by the advertisers against the highbrows who do not consume. That is one of the reasons for the decline of the prestige of culture.

Another reason : in the nineteenth century only the few could read. In 1870 only one in four could read. Culture was confined to the few, and it had therefore a snob value. Now we have had seventy years of popular education. Everybody can read. Culture is in theory made available for everybody, because of their mastery of the art of reading. Also, all can hear music on the wireless, and all can in theory go to picture galleries. And the masses have found to their astonishment that really there is nothing in this business of culture after all. And it is true—there *is* nothing in it for the masses : because you cannot, just by learning to read, be made free of the world's great literature. ˊYou cannot, just by being able to see, be made able to appreciate the world's great pictures.

What was more to the point, culture did not give the masses power, cause them to be promoted at the office, increase their salaries, or improve their personalities. It did not enable them to get on better with their wives. What a gigantic swindle was this culture that had been put over on them. Culture, in fact, in being made available for and being found out by the masses, lost its prestige.

I will mention one or two more reasons. One is speed and movement. We are the most mobile generation that has ever existed. Constantly we are going from place to place. We have brought up a generation of young people who apparently think that any place is better than the place in which they happen to be, and therefore are constantly in transit *from* the place in which they happen to be. If the movement takes place in a motor-car, they are practically in heaven.

Now, in a motor-car you cannot read, write, think or even rationally converse. You sink into motor-coma, which is neither sleeping nor waking, but a condition in which one has lost most of the attributes of humanity. Large numbers of persons have identified the good life with this condition, and as a consequence spend large slices of their lives in motor-coma in continuous transit about the face of the globe, for all the world as if they were parcels.

If you look back over the great men of the past, they were by our standards practically stationary. Their bodies were fungus-rather than meteor-like. All the men I have most admired in the past, Socrates, Haydn, Mozart, Kant, Vermeer, moved about, I suppose, a bit ; Mozart when he was a child, quite a lot ; but by our standards, how small was their range of movement. By our standards they stayed to all intents and purposes in one place, and therefore they grew culturally and intellectually to bigger heights than we do, just as a tree grows larger than a man because a tree has the sense to stay put.

One final reason. The intellectuals of our time have been at war within themselves, mainly for political reasons. We have, almost all of us, been on the Left. Most of us, especially the younger, have been strongly influenced by Marxism, and we have known that the conditions under which we could write and produce, even the conditions under which we could read learn and appreciate, were conditions made possible for us only by an unjust social system. Our leisure, peace and tranquility, the books we read, the concerts we attended, were only made possible for us under this system, so we believed, by the toil of the working masses. We were living, in other words, and most of us knew it, in an ivory tower, whose base was rooted in the inequality of social injustice.

If we were to write at all, we must take advantage

of that ivory tower. But in so writing, we all in a sense felt that we were benefiting from, and therefore helping to perpetuate, the very injustices against which our spirits and our writings protested. Thus we were at war against ourselves.

In an extraordinarily illuminated essay, entitled *The Ivory Tower*, Virginia Woolf makes precisely this point. We were not united within ourselves ; we were separated from one another ; an army of rootless, detached individuals, joined by no tap root to nourish us with the masses, playing a lone hand against the society in which we lived. Who was it who said, " Writers of the world, unite, you have nothing to lose but your brains " ? And yet we could not unite. So it was that we turned and befouled those very qualities by reason of which we were elevated above our fellows ; befouled our own good sense, our good taste, our intellectual ability, and thus was born that treason to which I have already referred, the treason of the intellectuals protesting against intellect, of the cultured decrying culture.

These, then, are some of the reasons for the contemporary decline of culture.

The situation that resutls seems to me to be a fundamentally unhealthy one, and the first point I want to put to you, looking to the future planning of the world after the war, is that, short of two conditions which I shall mention, that situation will not only persist but will be intensified.

Let us look forward for a moment to the world after the war. Let us suppose that all goes for the best in the best of all possible worlds. War, we will suppose, is not an immediately threatening possibility. We will suppose further that we have turned the economic corner of capitalism, and that under some form of benevolent socialism or some form of mixed socialism-capitalism, the kind of thing that Herbert Morrison has been advocating, we have removed the fear of want and insecurity from the great majority of people in this country.

Conceive it, if you like, as a Beveridge world, in which most of the dull and drudging toil has been removed from the shoulders of men and women, who are assured of comfort and a financial competence in return for four or five hours machine-minding a day. Theirs, then, is dull, routine work, making little demands upon their faculties but giving them a good living wage, giving them comfort and security, and eating up only four or five hours of their waking life in return.

What are they to do with the enormous tracts of leisure thereby placed at their disposal? Given the existing attitude to culture, given to the fact that we belong to a community in which culture is in decline and the intellect suspect, how are the masses, emancipated for the first time from economic want and insecurity, going to spend their time? Consider the really terrifying prospect.

I think I can see an England in which whatever land is left over from cultivation is covered with a network of golf courses and tennis courts. Our roads will be covered with a solid mass of metal, composed of cars stretching from John o' Groats to Land's End wedged together in a single stationary and inextricable jam.

Our coasts will be ringed with a continuous series of resorts, in which jazz bands will discourse negroid music to tired sportsmen and their over-nourished wives. A deluge of news warranted not to arouse thought and carefully chewed so as not to excite comment will descend on the defenceless heads of the community. There will be a crop of those many aspirins for the sick headache of humanity—Christian Science, astrology, theosophy, Oxford groupism, spiritualism and so on ; all these will flourish and multiply and be cultivated inordinately. I can see long lines of women following Great White Masters out into the desert. .

In the end, the boredom will become so appalling that men and women will be driven to one of two alternatives : (1) to make life hard and difficult and dangerous again, in despair of tolerating the boredom of mass-produced creation-saving amusements ; (2) the masses will lose their human birthright of freedom and become robots, wholly dependent upon and debauched by cross-words, football pools, dirt tracks, dog tracks, dance halls, radio, the cinema, Southend and Blackpool, and all the other devices which it will then pay commercial organisations to invent, in order to exploit the vast leisure and increasing wages of an industrially emancipated but spiritually enslaved proletariat. In other words, Aldous Huxley's Brave New World ! That, it seems to me, is the most probable line of development, given the existing decline of culture, unless my two conditions are satisfied. That brings me—since I take it for granted that we wish to avoid either of these two contingencies—to my two conditions.

In order to introduce the first one let me say a word about the contrasted functions of the State in the past and in the present. I notice that all the great civilizations of the past have known and acted upon **an** important truth. That truth is that man does not **live** by bread alone, but that he also lives by circuses ; **that** he lives, in other words, not only to work but also **to** play. I here use the word " play " not merely in **the** sense of rapidly altering the position of one's body **in** space, or of whacking, hitting, stroking and **pushing** round bits of matter about with long straight ones, **or** watching other people hitting, whacking, stroking **and** pushing. I use it in the widest sense to mean, **first,** the erecting at public expense of noble works **and** monuments, in which the spirit of the civilization **will** receive permanent embodiment, so that future **ages** will marvel at the skill of its craftsmen, at the **vision** that inspired its artists, at the public spirit **which** actuated its rulers.

I use it, secondly, to mean the staging of shows **and** ceremonies in which citizens may take delight and **feel** at one with their community when their work is done, so that by virtue of their participation, they may **be** lifted out of themselves and imbued with a gaiety **of** spirit greater than they individually could have experi- enced, and given a sense of the beauty and passion **of** life keener and more vivid than they could realise **by** their own unaided vision. I suggest to you that all **the** great civilisations of the past have regarded the provi- sion of " play " in that sense as part of the duty of **the** State.

So you get the Colosseum in Rome, the Parthenon **in** Athens, the Hanging Gardens of Babylon, the amphi- theatres, the baths, the palaces, the law courts **of** Roman antiquity, all permanent monuments to **the** greatness of a civilisation which found its most appropriate expression in noble works.

Then with the coming of Christianity, you see the spirit of the age finding its most appropriate outlet in the construction of great works of piety, in the cathedrals. (Why is it, by the way, that whenever one is moved in this our age to express one's admiration for some monument or building, it turns out nine times out of ten or nineteen times out of twenty to be several hundred years old? Why is it that the greatest commendation we can make of our small towns, villages or inns, is that they are " unspoilt ", meaning not yet spoilt by us?)

It seems to me that in the shows and ceremonies which the mediaeval State promoted, in the folk dancing and festivals and harvest merry-makings which came from the people themselves, no less than in the churches, buildings, Guild Halls and cathedrals, you get a notable expression of the great truth that man cannot live by bread alone, that he must play as well as work, and that the promotion and direction of his playing is a State duty and a State charge.

About the end of the eighteenth century and the beginning of the nineteenth, there is ushered in by the industrial revolution a new conception of the State and of the functions which it might legitimately assume ; a conception which embodied one of the most damnable heresies that has ever militated against the happiness of mankind, namely, the conception that limited the State's activities to the economic. That it should pay now became the one criterion that it was legitimate to apply to the activity of the State, pay, that is to say, in terms of hard cash accruing directly to the State, or pay by contributing to the accumulation of hard cash by private persons, who held prominent positions in. the State. "Brass," as they call it in the North, became the sole standard of value and its increase the sole ground for State action. It followed that to spend public money on non-economic purposes was to waste it. Even expenditure on education and health was defended on the ground that it paid—a man was a better clerk if he knew the multiplication table, a workman was a more lucrative employee if he was not always going sick.

Under the influence of this conception, architecture, music, the theatre and the provision of public shows and ceremonies have all fallen into desuetude.

Under its influence we take it then for granted that our State should *not* build Pyramids, Colosseums, Parthenons, Cathedrals or palaces ; it seems to us wholly in the nature of things that it should *not* provide out of public funds a State Theatre or a State Opera House where the best dramatic and musical art of the age could be exhibited for the delight and ennoblement of citizens— or did, until the war came, and brought something in the nature of a cultural awakening.

And what did the war show us, when it did come ? It showed us, first of all, that over large parts of England there was not even a hall in which a concert could be given or a speech could be made. If it has fallen to your lot, as it has to mine, to go about the country making speeches for the Ministry of Information, you will have found that in many towns there is nowhere to speak except in those awful cinemas, where the audience sits like a lot of sponges, accustomed to absorbing and giving nothing back as they hold hands in the dark. There are no halls, and incidentally there are no theatres. It is estimated that prior to the war, four-fifths of the people of this country had never seen a live flesh and blood play ; there were no theatres in which they could see them.

There was one other truth the beginning of the war disclosed, and which is still valid. It is this. That most citizens, when they come to the spending of their leisure, find that they really know very little about the art of living, because nobody has ever told them about the art of living, or suggested to them that it was an art. How, then, could they have learned it ? Here we are spending four-fifths of our waking hours getting the means to make life possible, and with only one-fifth left over for living, so that to this, the art of life, the most important of all the arts, we have brought tired brains and jaded nerves, and the fag ends of days devoted to getting the means to make our life possible.

Here, then, are two results of the limitation of the State's activity to the purely economic :

(1) No material environment in which culture could be conveyed : no halls, no theatres, no concert rooms.

(2) People have been thrown helpless, when their leisure came, upon their own resources, and have therefore never developed any taste for the things that appertain to the mind and the spirit.

I suggest to you that from these two main by-products of our individualist civilisation you can derive two lessons pointing to what the Socialist State, when it comes to plan for the people, should do in the matter of culture. First, that it should resume the traditional function of the great States of the past, the function of deliberately supplying circuses as well as bread, i.e.

·deliberately providing for the cultural needs of the people. Secondly, the function of deliberately educating the people as a whole, so that they can take full .advantage of the opportunities it provides.

I would not suggest that as a result of the learning ·of these two lessons you will have in any sense of the word a cultivated people. It may be the case that most people are incapable of culture in the sense in which I began by defining it. It may be the case that only one out of ten of human beings is a potential intellectual, and that that percentage holds irrespective of class or opportunity.

I say that because of a book I was recently reading by a statistician, inevitably an American. He had spent his time collecting statistics as to the pursuits, avocations and mode of life followed by undergraduates at Oxford University at three distinct periods: (1) Just before 1840, when Oxford was still an aristocratic preserve; (2) About 1900, when Oxford had been invaded and was largely populated by the middle classes; (3) In 1937 when, a very interesting fact, nearly half, some 38 per cent., of undergraduates came from working-class homes.

The author had mapped out the specifications of two different kinds of life—one the normal, the other the intellectual. The normal life was that of the undergraduate who played games, got tight, ran after women, and did as much or as little work as was necessary to get through his schools and stay at the University. The other was the life of the cultivated man, the intellectual, who read hard, attended debating societies, discussed and exchanged ideas, went to concerts, concerned himself with art, philosophy, politics—availed himself, in short, to the full of the cultural opportunities that Oxford offers to intelligent young men.

The statistics showed the respective numbers falling within the two classes, and the interesting point about them was that the relative percentages of the under-graduates falling in the two classes scarcely varied, they remained about constant when Oxford was wholly aristocratic, largely middle-class and nearly half working-class. There were always about ten normals to every one intellectual. I mention the point here because it may be that we are glimpsing a fundamental division between mankind, the division between normals and intellectuals.

What I think is important—and here I come to the second lesson—is that every man and every woman should be given the chance of showing whether he is an intellectual or not. This means that everybody should be given by his education the chance of showing whether he has it in him to appreciate and to enjoy the spiritual, aesthetic and intellectual values which I have associated with the word culture.

This, of course, is not the present situation.

At the moment, broadly speaking, we have two distinct intellectual ladders. The first intellectual ladder has quite a number of rungs: the nursery school, the nursery governess, the kindergarten, the preparatory school, the public school, the university. The second one has only two rungs: the elementary school, the upper forms of which are sometimes dignified by the name of Senior School, and at eleven, if you are lucky, the secondary school.

One leaves the first educational ladder at 22, to find

the gates of all the professions and the windows of all the cultures open to one. Beginning as a doctor, lawyer, clergyman, school-master or lieutenant, you may end up a Harley Street specialist, a judge, a bishop, a head master, a general or a Blimp.

You leave the second educational ladder at 14. Beginning as an office boy, a newspaper boy, an errand boy, a pit boy or a shop assistant, you may end up a clerk, a miner, a mill hand, a shop-keeper or on the dole.

The two ladders lead, it is obvious, to two totally different lives.

Did anybody notice the interesting figures recently given in the *Manchester Guardian*, in a review of a book by Dr. J. F. Ross, entitled *Parliamentary Representation*, showing the educational ladders up which our Governors and M.P.s had climbed? The number of people in this country who go to public schools is 2 per cent. of the population. The number of M.P.s who come from public schools is 56 per cent. That is, 56 per cent. of M.P.s represent educationally 2 per cent. of the population. The number of people in this country who go to secondary schools is 5 per cent. The number of M.P.s from secondary schools is 21½ per cent. The percentage of the adult population going to neither public nor secondary schools but to elementary schools and only to elementary schools is 93 per cent. The number of M.P.s from elementary schools is 22½ per cent. of the total number. Thus, one of the main effects of the two ladders is to produce a totally disproportionate class apportionment of our governors. The Civil Service, I imagine, would in its higher ranks show very similar percentages.

If you are thinking of the planning of a Socialist State after the war, you can only avoid the advent of a Brave New World, of which I adumbrated a brief sketch earlier in the lecture, by doing two things :

(1) Saddling your Socialist State with the obligation to resume the function of the great States of the past, i.e. the function of providing public shows and ceremonies for the entertainment and elevation of the people ; and

(2) Substituting educational ladder for the present two—one educational ladder upon which we shall all set foot, and up which we shall climb just as far as our abilities will take us, irrespective of the bank balances of our parents.

A question which might very well be asked at this stage is : Why all the fuss ? I reply with another. I take it for granted that we revolt against Aldous Huxley's picture of a well-fed proletariat, living the lives of happy machines. But why do we ? What in the last resort is the case for culture in a community ?

Here, for the first time, I find myself on familiar territory. I ask myself this question : In what respects do human beings differ from and excel the beasts ? In swiftness or ferocity ? Obviously not. The deer is swifter, and the lion is fiercer. In size and strength ? Not at all. We give way in both to the whale and the elephant. Sheep are more gentle ; tortoises more patient ; beavers more diligent ; bees more co-operative ; the ants run the corporate state much better than any fascist. Our bodies are ridiculously ill-equipped for the business of existence. They survive in babyhood only with care and difficulty. They are the prey of innumerable diseases. Owing to their enormous complexity they are always going wrong, and they are so badly equipped against the vagaries of the climate that it is only by clothing ourselves in the skins of other animals that we survive at all.

In patience, endurance, size, swiftness, strength, some one or other of the animals has us beaten every time ; some one or other is tougher, longer lived, more enduring, more co-operative, more diligent. Yet these are precisely the qualities upon which, partly under the influence of Fascism and partly under the influence of competitive capitalism—here the squirrel beats us ; how much better a hoarder he is than even the most diligent capitalist—we have come to pride ourselves. Partly under the influence of Fascism and partly under the influence of competitive capitalism, human beings seek to excel in qualities in which the animals have them beaten every time.

In what then do our distinctive characteristics consist ? Broadly speaking, they are three :

(1) Reason. Man alone seeks to probe the secrets of nature, to meditate upon the purposes of life. Man alone is moved by curiosity and has a disinterested desire to know. One might almost define a cultivated man as one who is interested in matters which cannot possibly advantage him personally, and evolves as the result of his *disinterested* interest science, philosophy, history, literature and all that body of knowledge which constitutes our cultural inheritance.

There is also, of course, that use of reasoning to apply scientific knowledge to reach practical results ; hence the triumphs of applied science, the electric light, the motor car, anaesthetics, X-rays, and also the aeroplane, the bomb and poison gas.

(2) Secondly, there is the moral sense. Every individual except man acts as he does because it is his nature so to act. It is only in respect of a human being that you can ask the question, not " How does he act ? " but " How ought he to act ? " It is only in respect of a human being that you can raise the question, " Ought he not to do what is right and eschew what is wrong ? "

(3) Thirdly, there is the sense of beauty ; man recognises and responds to beauty in the natural world, and creates for himself images of beauty in sound, or paint, or steel, or film, or words. Just as we owe to man's reason, philosophy and science, to his moral sense, and justice, so we owe to his sense of beauty, art. And from this point of view, not less important than the power to produce is the ability to recognise and respond to what is beautiful. You can be a cultivated and a cultured man even if you have not got an ounce of creative capacity yourself. I think the sense of beauty is in the last resort akin to the sense of right and wrong. The good life has a beauty of its own in virtue of which it may be represented as a work of art.

For beauty in art and literature affects our lives, making us more sensitive to and considerate of the feelings of others, helping us to find more interest in life precisely in so far as we bring to it minds which are fuller and more critical, and enabling us to see in the world more beauty, more passion, more scope for our sympathy and our understanding than we saw before. In other words, the effect of great literature and art is to be measured by its effect upon us as persons, who are brought into contact with it.

In developing these human characteristics, reason in

science and philosophy, morals in conduct and the sense of beauty expressing itself in sensitiveness to greatness in literature and art ¡and the demand to know what great men and women have said and thought memorable about life—we are developing the distinctive characteristics of humanity, those in respect of which we differ from and excel the beasts.

If you are asking yourselves, then, in what does a cultivated society consist, the answer is that it is one which encourages the development of the three faculties in which our specific humanity consists.

In the long run the purpose of a Socialist State, which is also the criterion by which its excellence is to be judged, lies precisely in its ability to provide those conditions in which a man can realise these distinctive characteristics of humanity, can in fact become fully and completely a human being. It is by this same criterion that we must condemn all the States of the past, seeing that most of their citizens have not been fully and completely human beings, have, in fact, been aborted in respect of their humanity.

As I was saying, it seems to me that it is only in a Socialist State that you can expect the community, through its chosen representatives, to accept the obligation to provide the conditions in which most human beings can become cultured, of providing also the education which will allow them to take advantage of the conditions.

BUDGETING IN THE POST-WAR WORLD

By JOAN ROBINSON

IT is impossible to discuss the Budget as a thing in itself. It expresses a point of view about the relations between the Government and the rest of the economy —a view of the relations of the State to industry and trade. Up till very recent times the prevailing view was that there is a certain sharply defined sphere of Government activity, and that all the rest must be left to the "free play of individual enterprise". On this view the State was regarded as one corporation existing side by side with other corporations and private citizens. Accordingly, it was subject to the same financial rules as apply to an individual. It was from this point of view that the maxims of Sound Finance grew up. The first rule of Government finance was that the Budget should balance, that all outlays should be covered within the year by tax receipts. For the Government to get into debt to its citizens was regarded as being just as dangerous and imprudent as for one citizen to get into debt to another. Indeed, much more so. For there was never any objection (quite the contrary) to one citizen or corporation borrowing from the rest, for capital investment. With a few minor exceptions the State was not expected to make investments. And it must confine itself to living within its income.

War-time borrowing was only excusable as an emergency measure, and the reduction of war debt in the
subsequent period of peace was regarded as a worthy
ideal. In peace-time the sharp division between State
activity and private activity was expressed in the
ideal of the balanced Budget. Let the Government
balance the Budget, and private industry will do all
the rest.

But nowadays the behaviour of the private sector is
under criticism. Not only members of the Fabian
Society, but practically everyone in the country, except
Sir Ernest Benn, is dissatisfied with the record of the
private sector and is looking more and more to the
Government to set it right. The most striking, though
by no means the only criticism of the system that we
lived under between the wars was the enormous
wastage of potential wealth, and of life and happiness,
caused by the failure of the private sector to maintain
full employment. The inefficiency of the private sector, of which unemployment is the most glaring
example, must be corrected. How is our view of the
Budget affected by this ? It is drastically altered. For
the wastefulness of the private sector has led to a
general demand that the State should widen its sphere
of activity. Since private enterprise does not make
use of all the resources of the country—in manpower,
land and equipment—the State must take the responsibility of using them for good purposes. This new
conception of the duties of the Government is very
widespread. Even the champions of the independence
of industry accept it. The Federation of British Industries declare, " It may be that the Government will
nave to consider the need of expenditure upon public

works in the national interest, in order to provide an outlet for industry when the immediate post-war activity is slackening ".*

And the manifesto of the 120 industrialists states :

"Government and local authority schemes of work which will have real national value can and must be prepared to relieve unemployment in periods of trade setbacks. These schemes would be confined to 'public' work, i.e. new roads, water supplies, housing, and the like. The equipment of Industry with up-to-date plant and machinery, however, is as much in the national interest as public works, and Industry will be entitled to obtain financial assistance for industrial schemes if our view is accepted that service to the community must be its first aim.

"For alleviating unemployment the State might be called upon to take, on suitable terms as to interest and repayment, a share of what would be an uneconomic risk for private Industry ; or at any rate render available adequate credit, which is normally liable to be much restricted in these times."†

These gentlemen have evidently come round to Keynes's view that in times of slump "the State should step into the shoes which the feet of the entrepreneurs are too cold to occupy". Their acceptance is grudging and not very wholehearted. But even this reluctant acceptance goes far enough to destroy the old conception of the narrowly confined duties of Government and to put in its place a new conception of the State,

---

* Reconstruction, A Report by the Federation of British Industries, p. 29.

† A National Policy for Industry, p. 9.

as the regulator of the national income as a whole. Yet in spite of this radical change, maxims based on the old attitude still float around and fog the atmosphere of all discussions of post-war problems.

The central theory of Sound Finance, the duty to balance the Budget, was buttressed by various notions which have by no means yet been swept away.

The first concerns the special nature of wartime expenditure. We are always being told the story of the man whose wife had to have an operation ; " Because he could find £200 in such a crisis, it doesn't follow that he can spend £200 a year on doctor's bills without going bankrupt." So, we are asked to believe, it may be necessary for the State to spend huge sums in war-time, but it certainly cannot go on spending in peace-time. This belongs to the view of the State as a corporation side by side with others. It is only plausible if we think of the Government as just one of the citizens of the country. The analogy of the man with the sick wife is apt enough applied to our dealings with other nations. Drawing on foreign capital to pay for war-time imports is like the man drawing on his past savings to pay for an operation. But applied to internal affairs it is just plain nonsense. The surgeon is as much a part of the family as the man and wife. The idea that a nation can bankrupt itself by employing its own labour and machinery to make goods for its own consumption is the kind of absurdity which arises from mixing up the conception of the State as a separate corporation with the conception of the State as an organ of the country as a whole.

Another buttress of Sound Finance is the notion that Government loan expenditure is inflationary and private loan expenditure is not. This idea has great vitality, for it seems to be strikingly supported by the facts. In war-time there is a huge Government deficit and there is perpetual danger of inflation. But it is the scale of the loan expenditure which is inflationary, not the fact that it is the Government which makes it. Inflation arises when there is an excess of demand for goods over the available supply. A lot of income is earned in filling shells and building tanks, which is spent on clothes and jam and lipstick. But the ships to carry sugar and wool are supplying armies in the field; the lipstick factories have been closed down. The labour is in the forces or is making munitions. There is more money to buy less goods. And so there is a tendency to inflation, which must be combated by rationing and saving. Too much expenditure in relation to supplies is inflationary—whether undertaken by the Government or by private citizens. Th biggest danger of inflation will come after the war, precisely from private expenditure out of new borrowing or old saving, if it is allowed to leap forward unrestrained before supplies are plentiful again.

The idea that Government borrowing is more inflationary than any other kind of borrowing is mixed up with a rigmarole about the Quantity of Money and particularly the note issue, which I am sorry to say was put about by the economists. As an economist I can only apologise for getting you into such a muddle about it. The main point is simple enough. If there is unemployment, more outlay will put men to work making more goods, and inflation can set in only when outlay runs ahead of production. It is not Government outlay that is inflationary, but outlay, whoever makes it, beyond the capacity to produce.

The next prop of the Sound Finance complex is the motion of the "crushing burden of the National Debt". This is another confusion which comes from mixing up the part of the whole. The taxes which have to be raised from citizens to pay interest on the debt are all paid out again to citizens who own the bonds. There are some disadvantages in having to raise a lot of taxes, which I shall return to in a moment, but the simple idea that a country is richer the smaller its debt is just another confusion between the nation and the individual citizen.

Another buttress of Sound Finance has by now completely crumbled away. This was the the famous "Treasury View" that Government outlay cannot increase employment even in a deep slump. I should like to recall to you the circumstances in which it was propounded. In 1929 Lloyd George was conducting an election campaign on the slogan "We Can Conquer Unemployment". His policy consisted of a programme of public works—roads, housing, improvements in the telephone service, afforestation, and so forth. The Government of the day published a White Paper, including a section by the Treasury, criticising the scheme. The sections of the other departments were signed by their respective ministers, but the Treasury section was not signed by the Chancellor, Mr. Winston Churchill. It was somewhat irregular to use H.M. Stationary Office for party election propaganda, and highly unconstitutional to commit permanent civil servants to a view on a party issue. But let that pass. What was the Treasury View? It was that public investment could not increase the total of investment, because there is a certain rate of investment which takes place in any case, and if the State makes more, private industry will make less. This amounts to saying that there cannot be a slump, for a slump is precisely a period when the level of investments falls. The Treasury View was that it is theoretically impossible to have a slump, so that there cannot ever be any case for Government action to cure a slump. It may seem unfair to dig up from the past an absurdity which has since been repudiated. Those who now hold the Treasury view of 1929 are in about the same position as those who believe that the earth is flat, and it may seem unkind to hold them up to public scorn. But we must remember that these ideas were by no means the harmless foible of a group of eccentrics. They had an extremely important influence on policy. It was these ideas which were used to justify the great economy campaigns of 1921 and 1931. When the last post-war boom had exhausted itself and falling prices and unemployment set in, we had the Geddes Axe. Again in 1931, when we were plunging down into a deep slump complicated by a foreign exchange crisis, we were subjected to a great economy campaign. Local Authorities were compelled to ease work on building schemes. Unemployment relief was cut and the Means Test imposed. An emergency budget increased taxation, and cut the pay of all public servants. (There was a certain poetic justice in the fact that a protest against these cuts by the Atlantic Fleet finished off the Gold Standard, which the National Government had been formed to save.) Private people, under a confused notion of a "national emergency", cut down their expenditure. Unemployment increased by leaps and bounds. If the public had not been doped with the doctrines of Sound Finance the political history of this country, and indeed, the whole development leading us into this war, would have been very different. It is necessary to remember this history, and never to forget the moral that we have learned from it. These ideas are like those weeds, of which the least scrap takes root again if it is left on the ground, and we must take care that every remnant of them is thrown on the bonfire.

Suppose that we have made a clean sweep of Sound Finance, what principles of budgeting emerge? First, as a minimum, which is now pretty widely accepted, the negative principle that when unemployment is threatening, taxation should not be increased, and expenditure should not be cut. As a slump develops, tax receipts fall of, and expenditure on unemployment relief increases. This automatic emergence of a budget deficit is to be welcomed, and no attempt should be made to prevent it. It does something to put a brake on the growth of unemployment, which, without such brakes, would grow indefinitely.

In this connection it is interesting to consider what we may call the Beveridge Budget. The social insurance funds constitute a sort of second budget. They are; fed by their own special taxes, the weekly contributions of the insured, which under Beveridge's universal scheme would amount to a general poll tax—a weekly payment of so much per head by the whole population, except those on benefit at any moment. And they are· fed by the so-called employers' contributions, which are a general tax on all output. And they are fed also by a subscription from the National Budget. Their expenditure consists of administrative costs and the benefits paid out. Now when unemployment increases, benefits paid out automatically increase. And not only benefits to the unemployed, but sick benefits as well, for health deteriorates with loss of income. Their receipts also automatically fall off, for fewer contribu- tions come in when more people are on benefit. Thus the Social Insurance Budget, just as certainly as the national Budget, develops a deficit as unemployment increases. And this also is to be welcomed.

In Sir William Beveridge's scheme the Social Insur- ance Budget is designed to balance when unemploy- ment stands at 10 per cent. of the present insured classes. When unemployment is at a higher level, it must borrow; when at a lower level it develops a sur- plus. I should like to make a brief digression on this figure of 10 per cent. Why was it chosen? It is clearly not chosen as a probable figure. For either we shall have some kind of employment policy after the war, or we shall not. If we do not, the figure of 10 per cent. is much too low to be plausible. Before the war un- employment varied between 15 per cent. and 20 per cent., and if nothing is done about it there are strong reasons to expect a still higher level of unemployment after the next post-war boom is exhausted. On the other hand, if we do have an employment policy we ought to be able to do much better than average 10 per cent. So that 10 per cent. cannot be Sir William's estimate of average unemployment. Nor clearly is it an ideal to aim at, for it would mean say 15 per cent. of unemployment half the time. It was chosen, no doubt (because some figure had to be chosen to set out the arithmetic of the Social Insurance Budget) as a moderate sort of figure—fairly pessimistic compared to the ideal objective of an employment policy, so as to avoid the change of optimism, and fairly optimistic compared to the record of the past, so as to avoid the charge of pessimism. In my opinion, it would be much better to choose a low figure for unemployment at the point of balance—say 3 per cent.—and to arrange contributions in such a way that the Beveridge Budget balanced with 3 per cent. unemployment. Then a deficit would develop with every increase of unemployment above 3 per cent. The contributions, which themselves restrict employment by reducing spendable income, could then be correspondingly less.

Let us return now to the National Budget. We have seen that the minimum proviso of the doctrines that take the place of Sound Finance is that no attempt should be made to prevent the deficit which emerges in a slump by increasing taxes, or by wielding axes. But this is merely negative.

Another idea which is often put forward is what we may call semi-sound finance—that is the idea that the Budget should not balance annually, but should balance over a long period—say ten years. Expenditure should exceed tax receipts in times of bad trade, so as to help to keep up the level of employment, and in times of boom there should be a surplus to pay off the debt incurred in the preceding slump. This idea seems to me not to go far enough. The very fact that there are booms and slumps shows that there is a chronic wastage 'of resources. There is never full employment in an ordinary boom (a post-war boom may be exceptional) and obviously there can never be more than full employment. In a slump there is a great deal less than full employment. The average, good years with bad, is less than full empolyment. Between the wars, unemployment varied between one and three millions, and the average was more than two millions. This is the wastage of resources that must be prevented. To have a deficit in the slump is very right and proper, but the boom in which it would be right to have a surplus will never come. Thus I do not think semi-sound finance will meet the case.

We seem then to be led to the conclusion that State expenditure should normally exceed tax receipts. If we agree that when resources are wasting in idleness it is the business of the Government to see to it that they are put to good use, then we must agree that State expenditure should be at whatever level is necessary to see that resources are employed, and if this means a continuous excess of outlay over receipts the nonsensical doctrines of Sound Finance must not deter us from accepting it.

But even when we have cleared Sound Finance out of the way—when we realise that the National Debt is not a real drain on the nation's resources—we may still feel that there is something wrong in endlessly piling up paper claims on the wealth of the nation in the hands of a group of the nation's citizens—in fostering the growth of a rentier class whose only claim on society is that they happened to be well enough off to save while loan-expenditure was going on. I think there is a great deal in this view. The burden upon the rest of the community of rentier incomes can be very much reduced by lowering the rate of interest, and by taking interest-free loans by "creating money", as the phrase is. All the same, the accumulation of rentier wealth would go on. If this is an evil to be avoided, what are the alternatives? One would be to refrain from having a national development policy— to allow the misery of unemployment to spread over us again, and to waste all the potential real wealth that unemployed resources might produce. Against this, any evil that there may be in a growing National Debt is obviously trival. If there is no other way of getting the job done, continuous Government loan expenditure is clearly to be preferred, rentiers or no rentiers. In there another alternative? Yes. To carry out plans of national development, and to cover the whole cost out of current taxation. This would mean cutting down private consumption, and would lead to a higher level of Government outlay. For the taxes would not only check the saving of the rich, but also their consumption, and the resources released from private luxury consumption would have to be disposed of to the social benefit, as well as the resources otherwise unemployed. It would be impossing collective forced saving upon the community in place of private saving. This is certainly the correct policy in wartime. Sound finance, in countenancing war-time borrowing, made an exception precisely where it is not justified. In war-time taxation is to be preferred to borrowing, because it cuts down consumption and releases resources for the war. But in peace-time a level of government outlay from tax receipts adequate to maintain employment would involve a level of taxation that would rapidly dry up the springs of private enterprise. In peace-time, such a system is not compatible with any kind of "half-way house". It would either break down or lead quickly into a fully socialist system. Definite finance is therefore a policy of reform as opposed to revolution. It means borrowing the savings of those who are rich enough to save instead of confiscating them. The defenders of the *status quo* take up a very dangerous position for themselves if they stand upon Sound Finance. A budget deficit is their best friend.

There is another problem raised by the overthrow of Sound Finance, of quite a different nature. This arises from the mentality of Treasury officials. Hitherto they have been brought up to believe that spending public money is a Bad Thing—to grudge every penyy, to pare every cheese. However much we may grouse and complain, we must admit that they fulfil a necessary function. It is desirable that all expenditure should pass through a fine sieve, that there should be no avoidable wastage, that society should get the best possible real return from its real resources, and, since calculations must be made in terms of money, this can be ensured only by a close check on money outlay. For this reason it seems to me that the overthrow of Sound Finance entails certain dangers. If we bring up a generation of officials to believe that a deficit is a Good Thing, they may become demoralised. The traditional stinginess of the Treasury is a national heritage which we must be careful not to dissipate.

For this reason I am strongly in favour of what is usually, though inaccurately, called a Capital Budget. The Capital Budget really means a plan of national loan expenditure. I believe that this should be separated from the ordinary Budget, and the evil name of a deficit should not be attached to loan expenditure which is deliberately made to build up the real wealth of the nation. Of course expenditure from loans should be scrutinised with as much care to avoid waste as expenditure from tax receipts. But I feel that it would be much easier to maintain the double attitude, that spending is a Good Thing and waste is bad thing, if there was a sharp distinction between borrowing for the positive purpose of building up national wealth and borrowing as a negative result of failing to balance the income account. Moreover, there is much more involved than a mere verbal point, for a Minister in charge of a national development plan would become something more than a Chancellor of the Exchequer, and a new branch of his department would develop where a new set of officials could be trained up in a new atmosphere, free from the fog of Sound Finance which will cling at least for a generation to come in the chambers of the Treasury.

Supposing that we have such a Minister of National Development, what would be his task? First of all, his policy must be framed not in terms of money, for there is no limit at all to the money that could be put at his disposal. It must be framed in terms of man-power, productive capacity and imported materials. It is these, not money, that set the real limit to national production. And he must take into his view not merely a narrow range of traditional government functions, but the whole development of the national economy. Merely to preserve full employment by doing some-thing or other to "make work" is not a rational policy. The true aim of policy should be to see that the whole resources of the nation are put to the best practicable use. A part of the national resources must be allocated to defence and administration, a part to current consumption, and a part to building up national wealth. The latter includes not only industrial, but also social investment such as building hospitals and schools and providing scholarships to increase the supply of doctors, nurses and teachers. And it cannot be strictly separated from what is normally regarded as consumption, as Mr. Churchill has said, there is no finer investment than putting milk into babies. Investment may be undertaken by private firms, by Local Authorities and public boards, or directly by the spending departments of Government.

The general allocation of resources and the division between the sphere of public, quasi-public and private enterprise involves all sorts of general political questions which I will not attempt to discuss to-day, when we are concerned only with the budgetary aspect of the matter. General policy, made up on doubt of a mass of compromises of all kinds between rival interests, will somehow or other settle a scale of priorities, and the business of our Minister is to implement that policy, and to see that the demand for the nation's resources is neither too great, so as to precipitate inflation, nor so small as to generate unemployment. At some times his task may be to curb private investment. This is likely enough to be the chief problem immediately after the war. Schools, hospitals and houses for the workers should take precedence over luxury flats, just as at present investment for war purposes takes precedence over inessential production. More normally, judging by pre-war experience, private enterprise fails to do enough, and must be supplemented by direct public investment, or encouraged by the provision of Government finance, if private management is preferred to direct public operation.

Taxation must be regulated primarily with a view to leaving enough, and not too much, purchasing power in the hands of the public to permit that level of consumption which will fit the general plan. In short, money outlay, public and private together, must be made to fit the allocation of real resources, and the primary decisions must be taken in terms of manpower, not of money.

This seems to me to be the minimum requirement for an employment policy that has any hope of success. And consequently, it seems to me the most essential change in budgeting principles that will be required in the post-war world.

What does our financial system look like on this basis? We have three separate accounts—the ordinary Budget looking after normal annual outlay, the Social Insurance Budget, and the Loan Account. The two first Budgets should be framed so as to balance when employment is at a satisfactory level, allowing a small margin for the irreducible short-term unemployment which is due to minor ups and downs in particular industries. Loan-expenditure should be framed so as to maintain employment at that level. When it fails, the two first Budgets would run into deficits. This would be a sign of failure in the plan. It must be remedied by more loan expenditure over the next period. and meanwhile the deficits on the normal Budget and the Social Security Budget should be allowed to run, and should be welcomed as putting a brake on the increase in unemployment. If the plan of loan expenditure has been too generously framed, or if private

investment or consumption outlay make an uncontroll-
able spurt, the plan must be cut down for the next
period. Meanwhile the surplus which emerges on the
two first accounts will be helping to check inflation.
It may also be necessary to have some quick-acting
anti-inflationary device to mop up purchasing power—
for instance, a purchase tax on inessential goods whose
rates could be raised at short notice. This should be
included in the ordinary Budget, and the proceeds applied to reducing the national debt. If we are really
going to have a full employment policy, we shall need
to have some weapon handy to combat inflation, in
case we overshoot the mark. But I do not think the
menace of inflation of this kind in peace-time is likely
to be so serious as in war-time. The vicious spiral of
wages and prices is another matter and must be tackled by other means. The first sign of the type of inflation we are now discussing is not a rise of prices, but
a running down of stocks. If stocks are sufficient and
if the statistics of stocks are available, it ought to be
possible to readjust the plan of loan expenditure before
a serious price rise sets in, and so to continue from
year to year sailing on an even keel.

Another aspect of budgetary policy which is of the
highest importance is its reaction upon the distribution of wealth and income. This is closely connected
with the employment problem. It plays an important
part in the allocation of resources between consumption and investment. The more equal is the distribution of income, the higher will be the level of consumption, and therefore, the smaller the scope for investment, both industrial investment and social investment in health and education. But we must also

consider the allocation of the total of consumption between individuals. How far is it possible to correct inequalities by budgetary means? Everyone agrees in principle that the tax system should be progressive— that a larger proportion should be taken from a higher income—though there is no accepted principle of just how progressive it should be. In fact, our pre-war tax system was regressive over the lower range of incomes. It has been calculated that a married man with two children paid a smaller proportion of his income in taxes the higher his income, up to £350 per year. Only above this range did progressiveness set in and the proportional tax burden on an earned income of £1,000 a year was little greater than the burden on £100 a year.* The regressive element in the tax system was due to indirect taxs—such as duties on tea, sugar and tobacco. Now that we have grown accoustomed to Income Tax on wages, it seems at first sight as though the right policy would be, when the time comes to reduce the total of taxation, to start at the bottom end and remit these indirect taxes so as to eliminate the regressive element from our tax system. But there is a very awkward problem here. The point of progressive taxation is that it takes a larger proportion from a higher than a lower income. By the same token, it takes a larger proportion from any additional income that an individual earns than from his whole income. We see this in the most striking way in the case of a man whose normal income is just below the exemption limit, and who has to pay tax if he works overtime. Instead of getting more money per hour for

---

*. See G. Findlay Shirras and L. Rostas, *The Burden of British Taxation.*

overtime, he may actually get less than for an hour of normal time. This naturally tends to discourage effort, and would do so still more in peace time than it does at present, when other motives and compulsions beside the desire to earn money are in operation. It applies not only to wage-earners, but the whole way up the scale. This sets a limit to the extent to which it is possible to equalise incomes by the system. For a thorough-going policy of redistribution it would be necessary to use other methods—price control, minimum wage legislation and educational reform to make opportunity more equal.

But of course the main inequalities of our system do not arise from unequal earning power, but from property incomes. Is there a similar limitation to a progressive tax system in that sector? We shall hear a great deal (we are already beginning to hear) about how taxation of profits is a burden upon industry, destroys enterprise and eats into capital. There will be a clamour to reduce taxation. "Wealth must be re-created before it can be redistributed", and so forth. What does all this amount to? To understand the argument we must break it up into two parts. There is first the argument that taxation falling on profits reduces the inducement to invest, and second, the argument that it reduces the funds for investment—first that it makes it not worth while to risk capital in investment, if you have got it, and secondly, that it leaves you with less capital to invest, even if you wanted to.

The first argument is mainly used in respect to Income Tax and Supertax. Income Tax it is said, goes on the principle: heads I win and tails you lose. If a risky investment turns out well, part of the proceeds go to the exchequer; if it turns out badly, the investor bears the loss. There is much force in this argument when rates of taxation are high. The difficulty could be overcome by introducing a new kind of tax into our system—a tax assessed on capital wealth, at rates which would normally be paid out of income. Such a tax would fall on wealth whether it was invested in safe or risky lines, or merely kept in the chimney, and would therefore not discriminate against enterprise. Another type taxation which reduces inequality with the minimum of deleterious reaction on enterprise is Death Duties. The argument that taxation of profits is dangerous because it checks enterprise can largely be met by altering the form of taxation.

How about the other part of the question? How far does taxation which falls on high incomes reduce the supply of capital available for investment? There is a great deal of confused thinking on this question. Capital equipment is made with steel and bricks and labour, not with money. The limit to the rate at which we can reconstruct and expand our capital wealth after the war is set by our skill and knowledge, our labour force and our facilities to buy imports, and by our rate of consumption—that is by how much of our real resources are devoted to providing for current consumption as opposed to increasing our stock of wealth. Finance does not set the limit. A "scarcity of capital" in the financial sense means something quite different. It means that there is a divorce between the ownership of investable funds and the people who are suited to undertake investment. Suppose that as a result of war-time taxation firms are left without reserves accumulated from past profits, and that the war-time savers, who have wealth to dispose of, are reluctant to lend to industry, so that new loans are hard to float, then there would be a "scarcity of finance ". It is often argued that high taxation creates this state of affairs, and it is argued that a remission of taxation would permit firms to accumulate funds, and to so make investment possible. Is this a valid argument against taxation which falls on profits ? I do not think so.

For there is no reason to suppose that just those firms who happen at any moment to be making the biggest profits are the ones most suited to undertake the new investment. A system of distribution of new capital according to who happens to have funds cuts entirely across any rational scale of priorities. The proper policy for "recreating wealth" is to consider what investment needs doing, to undertake direct wherever that is appropriate, and where private management is preferred to make State loans for approved projects. The divorce between owners of wealth and enterprising investors can easily be overcome by the nation as a whole taking over the function of ownership.

As far as this question of " scarcity of capital " is concerned, there is no reason why the tax system should not be just as progressive as we please.

We come back to the conclusion that our Chancellor of the Exchequer transmogrified into a Minister of National Development, must think in real terms, of man power and material, not in terms of money. He must consider not only the right total amount of investment, but also what kind of investment is most needed, and he must not allow the mythology of

Sound Finance to stand in his way. The pace at which we can progress towards prosperity and social justice is not set by finance, but by our resolution to get there.

A BETTER CIVIL SERVICE

By G. D. H. COLE

Attacking Civil Servants has long been a popular pastime ; and I have no wish to find myself a playmate in this activity with Sir Ernest Benn's Individualist League or with the *Daily Mail*. So let me say at the outset that I believe our permanent Civil Servants, at all levels from the highest to the lowest, to be pretty competent, honest and conscientious, and not at all sadistically disposed. I do not believe that they take a fiendish pleasure in devising forms for the rest of us to fill up; I do not believe they are habitual slackers; and I do not believe either that they are wicked bureaucrats, fanatically avoid of power. I have had a fair amount to do with them, over a good number of years ; and I must admit that, in their collective capacity, I do not love them. But emphatically these are not the charges which I think can be preferred against them with any substantial element of truth.

My charges are quite different, and are largely directed against the system, rather than against the

individuals who are its victims. I think that the
average highly-placed Civil Servant has too little
knowledge of people outside the narrow group with
which he ordinarily mixes in social affairs. I think he
is caught too young, and tamed too thoroughly in the
practice of a particular routine. I think he enjoys too
much security, under conditions which tend to make
him erect into an ideal the negative virtue of never
making a mistake. I think he is very apt to be the
kind of man who puts a high value on mere security,
and lacks all instinct for adventure. I think he suffers
under a departmental system of organisation which
breaks up responsibility into too small pieces, and
tends to make a virtue of avoiding it altogether. I
think he shares with many other professionals the
habit of clannishness and of feeling himself one of a
corporate group perpetually on its defence against the
rest of the world. And I think he exists under a
system of grading and promotion and of Treasury
supervision which is destructive of initiative for the
majority of those subjected to it, and often wrongly
selective in those whom it raises to the highest positions.

These are criticisms of the higher Civil Service as it
exists in time of peace, and in relation to its normal
duties. In wartime, of course, the Civil Service is
greatly diluted by " temporaries " of various types,
from " dollar a year" men seconded from trades and
industries as controllers of this or that, or as technical
advisers to controllers, to typists who fall a long way
below the normal civil service standards of accuracy.
among these "temporaries" are not a few members
of my own profession—the dons—and I should not be

surprised if my fellow-academics were found to have behaved quite as bureaucratically as the "regulars", and indeed to have displayed many of the same mental characteristics. For dons, like Civil Servants of the higher grades, are recruited largely from among cleverish, unadventurous persons who like a quiet life, set a high value on security, and regard the rest of humanity as, in Carlyle's famous phrase referring to the electorate, " mostly fools."

It is not, however, my purpose to devote this lecture to a discussion of the peculiarities of the Civil Service in wartime. What I am setting out to consider is the sort of Civil Service we shall want after the war, and in that connection what were the merits and defects of the Civil Service which we actually had up to 1939. If references to war conditions come into this lecture, they will be only incidental : my main concern is with the permanent—in technical phrase the "established" —Civil Service.

It is a great thing, which we take nowadays so much for granted as often to forget how great it is, that this established Civil Service of ours is for all practical purposes incorruptible. Not merely do its members not take bribes: they are for the most part continuously on their guard against much more subtle and insidious forms of corruption. If someone asks them out to dinner, they are very ready to ask themselves whether it is really for the sake of their *beaux yeux,* or from some ulterior motive; and they are even, a little apt to unduly suspicious of that part of the world which does not follow their own high calling. Or perhaps they are not unduly suspicious; for the ways of what is called "private enterprise" are dark, and the

guardians of the public virtue need to be careful not
to be beguiled. At all events, dishonesty among Civil
Servants is a very rare event; and, if I need say no more
in his lecture about the morals of the Civil Service, it
is because the moral qualities of its members, in their
official behaviour, shine like good deeds in a naughty
world.

They are clever too, as well as honest, these servants
of the public. In every grade, the standards required
of new entrants are high, in point of intellectual attain-
ments, in comparison with what is called for in most
walks in life. When they go wrong, it is not because
they are mutton-headeds, or unable to appreciate even
subtle intellectual points, but for some quite other
reason.

Is it, then, that there is nothing aims with our Civil
Servants, and that, if we love them not, it is only because it is in the nature of their calling not to be loved?
It is their mission to ensure that private persons, in
their dealings with the State, shall do, not as they
would do, but as they would be done by, and so that,
in Kant's phrase, whatsoever they do shall be in ac-
cordance with "law universal". They have to go by
rule, because they must show no favour to one man
as against another; and the rule, when we find it applied to our own case, commonly seems hard and in-
human, and often lacking in common sense. The Civil
Servant is essentially an applier of general rules to
particular cases; and it is in the nature of his duty that
he has no liberty to make exceptions. He is a trustee,
and not a dispenser of charity: an interpreter of laws,
and not their maker: a servant of servants—for Minister means servant—and not a master, at any rate in the

theory of the Constitution: a regular, and not an original source of power. If this is theory, and in practice the Civil Servant often becomes the master of the Minister he is supposed to serve, and even of the public that Minister is supposed to serve, how can he help it? He is the expert, who knows all the ropes; and what he knows best of all is that Ministers are but amateurs, who blunder sadly if he does not continually save them from themselves.

The relations between Ministers and Civil Servants are, indeed, at the very ear of the problem we are setting out to discuss. Broadly speaking, a Government Department has two distinct functions to fulfil. it has to see to the practical and orderly administration of an existing body of law, and of rules and regulations based on law and custom; and it has to play its part in the making of new laws or the amendment of existing rules and practices. Inevitable Ministers are much more concerned with the second than with the first of these functions. They may regard themselves as endowed with a mission to effect changes in policy, and yet be fully aware of their shortcomings as arbiters of administrative method. The typical Minister does not greatly interfere with the working of those parts of his departments' duties which are not immediately affected either by popular controversy or by proposals for legislative change. He leaves the running of such things mainly to the permanent secretary and his subordinates, and attends principally to those matters about which he is likely to be questioned in Parliament or, to have to take charge of for a Bill. The habit of shifting Ministers frequently from one office to another obviously makes for leaving the high Civil

Servants largely free to run the departmental machine as they please, subject to the knowledge that the Minister will be bound to interfere if their proceedings give rise to public protest or offend any powerful interest. It is very much the concern of most officials to avoid having the Minister's attention drawn to matters which they deem him, in most cases, ill-qualified to understand. An incautious reply by a Minister to a questioner in Parliament may upset their best-laid plans and cause an upheaval in their department; and a Minister, who knows the rules much less well than they do, is exceedingly apt, in judging the particular case on its merits, to overlook the endless repercussions of what may seem to be an obviously just or sensible judgment. They have to protect him against his own humane impulses, and in doing so to protect themselves against administrative complications which might land everybody in a mess.

There is no denying the force of the Civil Servant's case when he argues that it is dangerous to give the Minister his head. Yet this attitude of the custodian of orderly administration passes easily into the perversion in which it becomes sheer obstruction to change. What is, becomes because of the complications involved in changing it, to be identified with what ought to be; and this happens the more easily because of the unchanging rhythm of the high-up Civil Servants everyday life. From home to office, from office to club, where he hobnobs largely with other Civil Servants of his own standing, from club back to office, and from office to home, his life follows, in times of peace, a singularly invariable course. His job itself is not monotonous, in the sense in which monotony is the lot of the routine worker from day to day; but its rhythm is constant, even if there is variety in the things which he has to do. It would be remarkable if it did not make him, unless he has strong anarchistic instincts, conservative and averse from change, more apt to envisage difficulties than opportunities, and disposed to let well alone and to define "well" as meaning that which least disturbs the evenness of his days. That his work is interesting does not militate against this conservatism but may even exaggerate it; for he is not discontented with what he has to do, and has therefore no inner urge to get it altered. He has chosen his career with his eyes open, knowing its limitations as well as its privileges; and he is aware that he is most likely to be allowed to get on with his job in his own way if he does nothing that will cause him to be interfered with. Consequently, he fears, or even resents, a pariamentary question which touches upon his duties; and in priming his Minister with the required answer, or with the arguments to be used in debate, he is concerned mainly to afford no opening for further questioning, and to get away with giving as little information as will serve to keep the questioner quiet, and give the press no handle for comment that may set the public mind astir.

This kind of Civil Service is a product of the reforming zeal of the nineteenth century. It superseded a service very differently constituted, in which sinecurits held many of the most lucrative posts, and the more laborious minor offices were filled largely by favouritsim and nomination of the dependants of the great. Competitive examination was the new broom which swept the incompetents away, and enforced a high in-

tellectual standard; and the moral standard rose simul-
taneously with the intellectual, under the stern
governance of the preceptors of retrenchment and
reform. When this reformation was effected, the job
of the Civil Service was almost exclusively regulative,
rather than administrative: it was concerned much
more with seeing that certain things were not done
than with doing things in any positive sense. Apart
from the Post Office, which long remained anomalous
in its methods, it had no big service to manage save
that of tax-collection; and it came little into contact
wih the general run of men. Assiduousness and in-
tegrity were the qualities chiefly demanded of it:
human sympathy was not much in request, or business
capacity, or imagination, or even initiative in any of
its more creative forms. There were men in it who did
nevertheless display these qualities—for example, in·
the development of the public health services or in the
field of education. But even in these fields of activity
there was but limited scope for the creative powers.
The local authorities were the responsible executants·
of the policies prescribed or permitted by law: the Civil
Servant's function was rather that of ensuring that
they should not exceed their powers than that of pur-
ring them on to new endeavours. The overriding·
assumption was that Government ought to interfere
as little as possible, save to prevent abuse: hostility to
centralisation was exceedingly strong, and the belief·
in *laissez-faire* not indeed unchallenged but deep and·
pervasive throughout the influential part of society.

Since those days conditions have changed greatly in
more than one respect. For one thing, the social gulf·
between Ministers and Civil servants has narrowerd a:

great deal. Politicians have ceased to be mainly aristocrats; and Ministers, even Conservative Ministers, are nowadays a very mixed lot. As against this, the spread of secondary education has also altered the social complexion of the higher Civil Service; but the general effect has been to put Ministers and their departmental officials much more on a personal equality than they used to be, and therewith to give the greater expert knowledge of the official a stronger influence—the more so because the intricacy of administrative detail has immensely increased. This change in personal relations goes with a vast increase in the size of departmental staffs and in the range of duties falling within the scope of each department. The Civil Service has much more to do; and much more of its work is directly administrative and not merely supervisory. This, of course, applies very unevenly between deparments; and, over all, the Service still regulates much more than it administers. But there have grown up huge departments directly managing services which bring their officials into close and constant contact with the general public. The Ministry of Labour, with its Employment Exchanges and Training Centres, is one outstanding example; and the Assistance Board is another. But, apart from these, the general run of departments have many more points of contact with the public than they used to have. The Board of Trade is in much closer contact with business men over matters of industrial and commercial policy; the Board of Education is in much closer touch with the schools, including those outside the State system; the Ministry of Agriculture is in daily contact with farmers and dealers in farm produce; the Ministry of Health is in much closer touch·

than it used. to be, not only with the local authorities, but also with doctors, nurses, private builders, insurance companies, voluntary hospitals, and all manner of social service agencies. In a great many fields, there has grown up a new, and still rapidly developing, relationship between statutory and non-statutory agencies —an uneasy partnership in which the fuctions of the partners are subject to continuous and subtle alteration, both by law and in the gradual modifications of practice outside the law. Consultation with outside agencies have become a vital part of the technique of legislation and administration alike; and the wider the State's functions become, the more needful is it for this partnership of public and privates agencies to be developed.

One thing I feel sure of is that under these conditions it would be of advantage to have a regular practice of interchange between the Civil Service and the parallel service of local government. One occasionally meets even now officials who have had experience in both these fields; and it would be of advantage if there mere many more of them. Moreover, the interchange ought to take place not only among senior officials but also and above all among juniors in the course of getting their basis of experience. I am aware that there are pratical administrative difficulties in the way of this, as there are in the way of that unification of conditions in the local government service which is on its own account greatly to be desired. But these difficulties—in relation to pension rights, and so on—could be easily overcome if there were any will to deal with them; and I am sure the Whitehall official would be in many cases a better man if he had enjoyed some first-hand experience of the working of local government, and the local official a better man if he had served for a time under the conditions of Whitehall.

Greater mobility at all stages, but especially before the Civil Servant has settled down in mind and habit, is, I am sure, highly desirable, both from one central department to another and between central and local government. This could be brought about within the existing framework of the service, without any fundamental change. At the same time, a great deal more should be done to break down the rigidity of caste divisions inside the service, especially between those who enter it at different ages and with different educational backgrounds. It ought to be made much easier for those who enter as boys or girls, if they show promise, to rise to the highest positions; and these positions ought not, as they largely are to-day, to be reserved for University and public school men. In order to make this easier, there should be a provision on a generous scale of bursaries or fellowships, with the aid of which Civil Servants whose early education had been cut short could be sent for a year or for several years to a University equipped to receive them, for the purpose of improving their cultural and professional qualifications. I should much prefer this to the creation of an isolated Civil Service Staff College, which is now being advocated in certain quarters. The Civil Servant needs not more but less isolation from the rest of mankind, and will find better and wider opportunities in a University which handles students of all sorts than in a specialised institution—provided only that the University takes proper pains to equip itself for giving him what he needs. In addition to such longer full-time courses, there ought to be an abundant provision. of shorter "refresher" courses of all sorts and kinds, to meet the needs of men and women of different age, interests and capacities and to keep the Civil Servant up to date with the best current thought and experience in fields related to his professional work.

There are, however much wider questions than these to which we must give our consideration. Modern government is branching out not only on the social and administrative sides, with which I have been dealing so far, but also on the economic and business side. It is now pretty generally agreed that when the State takes over from private enterprise the running of any industry or economic service, the best way of running it is not through a civil service department staffed by regular Civil Servants recruited in the ordinary way and subject to the rigours of Treasury control, but rather through some sort of public board or corporation. Such bodies have been set up in quite considerable numbers in recent years, with widely varying constitutions and relations to the Government and to Parliament. In general, the practice has been to regard their staffs, from the top downwards, as being not Civil Servants, but simply employees of the particular boards or commissions concerned. No attempt has been made to introduce any uniformity of grading or salaries or other conditions of service; and there has been no formal security of employment, such as applies to the established branches of the Civil Service.

What this means is that in practice there has been growing up, side by with the recognised Civil Service, a second unrecognised body of public servants working under substantially different conditions, intentionally

CPSIA information can be obtained at www.ICGtesting.com
Printed in the USA
LVOW130310250812

295804LV00001B/327/A